TRAVEL 101

TRAVEL 101

A Band Director's Guide for Planning Student Travel

ANDREW M. YARACS

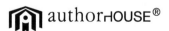

AuthorHouse™ LLC
1663 Liberty Drive
Bloomington, IN 47403
www.authorhouse.com
Phone: 1-800-839-8640

Published by AuthorHouse   02/07/2014

ISBN: 978-1-4918-6310-7 (sc)
ISBN: 978-1-4918-6309-1 (e)

Library of Congress Control Number: 2014902738

Table of Contents

Introduction

Have you ever thought to yourself "I wish I knew then what I know now" or "hindsight is 20/20"? When I think back to the day that I began planning my first band trip those sentiments are true. I wrote this book as a resource to help band directors who are interested in planning student travel opportunities. While the main focus is on travel and performance with a marching band the information can be adapted and applied to almost any group whether you're an orchestra or choir director, classroom teacher or club advisor. The content is a compilation of the things I learned through personal experience, networking with other band directors and dealing with several different travel companies over a fifteen year period from 1997 to 2012 as the director of the Butler High School Golden Tornado Marching Band in Butler, Pennsylvania.

Travel enriched the lives of my students and that opportunity provided an incentive for others to join the band and stay in the program. The chance to perform in front of millions of people and appear on nationally and globally televised parades in some of the nation's most prestigious events helped to foster a sense of pride and achievement. By writing a performance based travel component into the curriculum I changed a program that had never taken a trip into one that traveled yearly. To be in the band students had to audition and agree to all of the commitments on the schedule of performances including a yearly trip. If we had an expensive trip one year I planned a more economical trip the next year to compensate.

Our group numbered in the mid three hundreds with the staff, students and chaperones. The band was comprised of students in grades nine through twelve and ranged in age from fourteen to eighteen. We traveled throughout the United States and Canada and our trips focused on great performance opportunities with appearances on numerous regional, national and globally televised parades. We made multiple appearances at the Pasadena Tournament of Roses Parade, Macy's Thanksgiving Day Parade, Fort McDowell Fiesta Bowl Parade, Florida Citrus Parade, Philadelphia Thanksgiving Day Parade, Toronto Santa Claus Parade and Disney World Magic Music Days Parades. In addition we marched in the Kentucky Derby Festival Pegasus Parade, New York City Nations Day Parade, Chicago McDonald's Thanksgiving Day Parade, Disneyland Holiday Parade and the Pittsburgh Celebrate the Seasons and St. Patrick's Day Parades.

We logged thousands of miles on charter bus trips and cross country flights. Due to the size of our group we choose to charter instead of flying on commercial airlines when we traveled to Pasadena, California for the Tournament of Roses Parade and Phoenix, Arizona for the Fort McDowell Fiesta Bowl Parade. To accommodate the size of our group we had to charter two and sometimes three planes.

Our first chartered flight to the 2000 Pasadena Tournament of Roses Parade was the most memorable. Our travel company booked a Boeing 747 so we could fly everyone on one plane. We filled that plane with our students, staff, chaperones, superintendent, tour guide and family and friends from our community. That's four hundred and seventy seats! According to the airline we were the first high school band to charter a 747! We had to come up with over a half million dollars to get to Pasadena and the story of how we raised the money, prepared for the five and one half mile march, and chartered a Boeing 747 was featured in a half-hour documentary entitled "Here Comes the Band" that aired on HGTV prior to the 2000 Tournament of Roses Parade coverage.

With each trip I learned things I could do differently to improve the next. I was fortunate to have a well-established local student travel company plan my first trip. During that year we developed a comfortable working relationship and I grew to respect and trust their judgment in recommending the best experiences for my students. They ended up booking the majority of my trips and I learned much of what I know about travel planning from them. Some of the events that we participated in had a designated travel provider who was responsible for making arrangements for all the bands. Over the years I've worked with four different travel companies under those circumstances. These experiences were all different but positive and I learned from each of them. I found that the best way to get an honest opinion about an event I wanted to apply for was by calling band directors who had been there before.

My biggest concern when traveling was for the safety and security of the students. When seeking approval for each trip I presented a detailed plan to my administration and band parents outlining the precautions I have taken to provide a safe experience for the students. I had an outstanding team who shared in that responsibility including my staff, band boosters, school administration, my wife and numerous chaperones and volunteer nurses. Over the years I was also fortunate to get extra help from dozens of former band members who volunteered yearly to serve on my collegiate band staff.

During my tenure as the director of the Golden Tornado Band we received numerous invitations to travel overseas and perform however I choose to limit our trips to the United States and Canada. If you're interested in booking an overseas experience you should consult a company that specializes in international travel. A trip overseas will be more complex and require an even greater attention to safety and security.

How did I get so interested in group travel? As a teenager I had the opportunity to perform and travel with a local drum and bugle corps. I got to visit places I had never been before, see new sights, make new friends, and perform in front of new audiences. I learned the virtues of commitment, self-discipline, teamwork and responsibility as well as how to take care of myself away from home. Eventually I became the director of that group and spent several years planning their extended summer performance tours throughout the United States and Canada. This experience had a positive impact on my life and subsequently influenced my decision to incorporate yearly travel into my band program.

I hope you'll find this book helpful in planning years of enriching and safe travel opportunities for your students. Links to travel relate websites as well as sample letters, forms and diagrams are included in the resources section of this book. Feel free to copy and adapt them for your own use.

The Benefits of a Travel Program

➢ **Performance**—travel provides the opportunity to showcase your band in front of a new audience.

➢ **Pride**—students develop a sense of pride and accomplishment when invited to participate in a major event and serve as traveling ambassadors for their school and community. These events provide a great public relations vehicle for promoting your band and music education program as well as your school and community on regional, national or global television.

➢ **Recruitment & Retention**—travel adds an extra incentive for students to join the band and stay in the program. Students learn social skills, self-confidence, responsibility, commitment and the value of teamwork.

➢ **Interest & Integration**—public relations for your upcoming trip will foster interest about your students within the school and community. The extra amount of time students and teachers spend together provides a great opportunity for getting to know each other outside of the traditional school environment. Sharing time with fellow band students and students they will meet from other band programs fosters a sense of fellowship creating lifetime bonds and memories.

➢ **Educational Enrichment**—your students will see new sights, visit historic landmarks, meet new people and experience different climates as they travel across the United States or to a foreign country. The lessons they will learn from spending time away from home can be invaluable later in life and include responsibility, self-discipline, and teamwork, sense of community and basic life skills gained by living with others.

Butler Golden Tornado Band visits the Statue of Liberty—1997.
Photo by GroupPhotos.com

Butler Golden Tornado Band members get a chance to meet and visit with students from the other bands before the 2010 Fort McDowell Fiesta Bowl Parade in Phoenix, Arizona.
Photo by Jeff Groves

Getting Started

What's Your Objective?

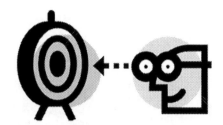

So you're thinking about planning a trip for your group. What's your objective? What do you want to accomplish? Are you looking for a performance opportunity with regional, national or global television coverage? Perhaps you're interested in taking your students to an instructional seminar or clinic, band competition, special concert or music festival. Maybe you just want to reward your students with a fun trip for an outstanding season? Whatever your reason taking a trip is a decision that shouldn't be taken lightly. Group travel presents challenges and will require extra time and effort on your part, your booster organization, parents and students as well as school approval. If you're married it may even affect the amount of time you have to spend with your spouse and family.

We've all heard stories about great student trips as well as those that didn't go so well. With careful planning and the help of an established travel company you can minimize problems and provide a safe, enjoyable experience for everyone. The rewards from a well-planned successful trip will far outweigh the challenges.

Before you start survey the interest and support you have for taking a trip with your staff, students, their parents, your band boosters and school administration. You'll want everyone onboard from the start.

A Planning Checklist

☐ Have a clear objective.
☐ Talk with colleagues who travel for advice on destinations, events, itinerary and a travel company they would recommend.
☐ Select a destination and event carefully consider the affordability and manageable travel distance as well as how it might fit within your school calendar.

☐ Check with other groups in your school that travel to avoid conflicts that may include the same students, travel date and fundraising.

☐ Plan early—at least 12 to 18 months in advance.

☐ Obtain the services of an established travel company.

☐ Contact references provided by your travel company.

☐ Create a budget. Consider length of trip, number of participants, and type of transportation, housing, meals, sightseeing, and extra security you want to include.

☐ Work with your travel company to create a plan within your budget.

☐ Review the itinerary with your staff and band boosters.

☐ Make final revisions to your plan and lock in your expenses.

☐ Get approval from your school administration.

☐ Establish a fundraising program.

☐ Create a payment schedule and accounting system to record student money from fundraising, donations and payments.

☐ Schedule meetings to inform parents and students about the trip. Provide information on the itinerary, cost, performance, fundraising opportunities, payment schedule and system for tracking student accounts.

☐ Keep parents and students up to date on trip information and fundraising via your website, handouts, e-mails, newsletters, and meetings.

☐ Get your community involved use newspaper, radio and television to share the word about your trip.

☐ Depending upon the magnitude and cost of your trip you may want to organize a committee to solicit corporate sponsors. Begin with a database of the major industries in your town and the places where your students' parents work.

☐ Place a thank you ad in your local newspaper to acknowledge contributions and donations from individuals and corporate sponsors.

☐ Develop a rehearsal strategy. Make sure you are aware of and plan for any requirements unique to the event you are attending i.e. music selection, special drill or parade block requirements etc.

☐ Have a backup plan. Expect the unexpected. Consider what you might do if circumstances arise that affect your performance, cancel your trip, require major decisions on student issues, housing, transportation, meals, or itinerary changes. Talk to your travel company about their "Plan B" for these situations.

☐ Assemble a 3 ring binder using clear plastic sheet protectors with all of the necessary documents related to your trip. Include bus, housing and chaperone assignment lists, administration, emergency and parent phone numbers, contact information for all of your services and vendors, copies of all contracts, itinerary details, maps, directions and performance information. Keep this with you throughout your trip.

☐ Do a follow-up report after your trip. Survey the students, parents, staff and chaperones regarding their experience. Itemize what went well and what didn't and create a list of the things that you can improve on future trips.

☐ Follow-up with your Travel Company. They will ask for your feedback on transportation, housing, meals, sightseeing, tour director services and security items.

☐ File your 3 ring binder with all of the financial records for your trip. This information will be a useful reference for planning future trips and also serve as a resource in the event questions arise after the fact regarding the trip.

Additional Items to Consider When Planning a Trip

> ➤ **School Restrictions**—As you begin planning, be aware of policies and or restrictions your school district may have regarding overnight student travel.

> ➤ **Spring versus Fall travel**—Most programs tend to favor spring travel since planning a year ahead often involves split classes and overlapping school years. How much school can your students afford to miss? Will the trip conflict with major testing periods? Should you plan a trip over school vacations or holiday breaks? Consider the climate and weather conditions for each destination.

> ➤ **Educational Value**—Every destination has potential educational value. With your staff and boosters discuss specific opportunities you would like to incorporate into the trip.

> ➤ **Bid process**—If your school policy requires the submission of competing bids for trip approval be sure to compare "Apples to Apples". All bids should reflect quotes on equal or similar items such as the location and quality of hotel, overnight security, transportation (consider age of the equipment), meals, sightseeing, admissions, performance opportunities, liability and emergency medical insurance, payment plan, complimentary packages, company history and cancellation policy.

The Application Process

To perform in a nationally televised parade, regional event, music festival, band competition or theme park you'll need to apply. Most applications ask for the director's bio, band size and instrumentation, type of auxiliary units, performance resume, group photo and contact information. You can often apply directly online at their website or download an application to complete and mail in. Make sure you take time and fill in the required information in a neat, concise manner and submit your application within the required deadline. A program coordinator, event chairman or music committee will review and evaluate your application and if selected will send you a formal invitation.

For the Pasadena Tournament of Roses Parade, Macy's Thanksgiving Day Parade, and Fort McDowell Fiesta Bowl Parade as well as a few others selections are made as much as eighteen months in advance. The application process is more involved and asks for the director's bio, current DVD of a field performance, letters of recommendation from college band directors, music professionals and or public officials, color photos of the band, auxiliary groups and sections that wear a different uniform, band size and instrumentation and your performance resume. You'll also need to provide documentation of your bands fundraising history and ability to raise the necessary money to get to the event.

When applying for any of these events it's a good idea to put together a professional looking portfolio. Each year they receive hundreds of band applications and you'll want yours to stand out from the rest. An attractive neatly packaged presentation can help sway the selection committee to invite your band.

In addition to selecting a few international bands the Tournament of Roses Music Committee strives to insure that a diverse cross section of the country is represented in the parade each year. To accomplish this applications are grouped together by regions of the country and evaluated accordingly. Their goal is to select the best representative band from each region. The Macy's Thanksgiving Day Parade follows a similar selection process. Once you have been chosen to participate in either of these events you cannot reapply to return again for several years. This policy provides more opportunities for different bands to participate. You can find links to their websites and a complete guide for preparing your application in the resources section of this book.

Why You Need a Travel Company

By the very nature of the job a band director is often quite good at problem solving, multitasking, working under pressure, making decisions and organizing, but when it comes to booking a trip you should enlist the services of a travel company. I've heard a few directors' boast about how they booked their band trip and did it much cheaper than if they would have used the services of a travel company.

Yes you may be able to save some money and planning a trip with a travel company will take some time and energy but going it alone can be detrimental to your career. Consider this. Do you have the resources and expertise to contract all the services and vendors required for a trip? Do you have the same buying power a travel company can provide? Can you deal with legal issues that might develop with service providers and vendors on a trip? Can you provide adequate liability protection for your students, school district and yourself? What would you do if your group was scheduled to come home but a snowstorm forced you to stay? How would you find enough available hotel rooms and pay for the extra meals and lodging for the night? A travel company has the means and resources to handle all of these issues. If you go it alone you may be subjected to questions from your administration or band parents regarding the trip finances and your accounting procedures. What would you do if they accuse you of shady dealings or creative bookkeeping? Protect yourself, do what's best for you and your students and hire an established travel company.

Aside from providing an expert to personally advise and guide you in planning your trip a travel company will provide liability protection, years of knowledge and expertise in working with the many services and vendors a trip requires i.e. transportation, housing, meals, sightseeing and admissions. They can recommend things they know will work well for your group and caution you about things that won't. If you encounter a problem with transportation, housing, meals, admissions, lost tickets, cancellations, or poor service on your trip it's their responsibility to handle the situation for you.

You can't predict what might go wrong on a trip but having the satisfaction of knowing you have someone on hand that can deal with the unforeseen is quite comforting.

Choosing a Travel Company

Some major events team up with a travel company and offer exclusive travel packages for the participating bands. This helps to ensure all groups receive a quality experience by providing comparable transportation, housing, meals and itinerary opportunities for each of them at a competitive price.

 If you need to find a travel company do your research carefully before making your decision. Consult with colleagues who have traveled for advice on a company they might recommend or suggest that you avoid. Consider the following before you sign a contract.

- How long have they been in the travel business and are they financially stable?
- Call their references and some of the bands they have worked with.
- How many full time employees do they have?
- How much liability insurance coverage do they provide? A sample certificate of insurance is provided in the resources section of this book.
- Is Medical Emergency Insurance coverage provided?
- Is trip insurance available?
- Do they belong to any business partnerships or national travel associations such as NTA (National Tour Association) and ABA (American Bus Association)? Links to their websites are provided in the resources section of this book.
- If you're traveling with an exceptionally large group ask if they have previous experience with a group of your size.
- Will they provide an experienced tour director from the trip's point of departure to its point of return?
- Will your tour director be housed at the same hotel as your group?
- Is there an emergency communication plan available to travelers and their families back home with an emergency contact person, 24/7 while your group is away?
- Is there an option available for direct collection and accounting of student trip payments to the travel company?
- What is their refund & cancellation policy?
- Will your trip include overnight hotel security on each floor, complimentary packages, and a director's pre trip inspection tour?
- Will a travel representative be available to make a presentation to your parents?

Hiring a travel company will shift liability from you, your school and boosters to a third party the travel company. You will work closely with a company for the better part of a year or more. If you feel you are not getting the attention to detail you deserve tell your representative about your concerns as soon as possible.

Preparing a Budget

Give your travel company a budget to work with. Decide what you want to include and the amount you're willing to spend per student. Base your figures on the type of hotel, overnight security, meals, method of transportation, admission fees, sightseeing items and number of days you plan to be away. Work with your travel representative to achieve your goals and stay within your budget.

The cheapest trip is not always the best trip or smartest way to go. Don't compromise the health, safety and security of your students just to save a few dollars. You're ultimately the person responsible for the group and will be held accountable by the parents for your decisions. Choose every aspect of your itinerary wisely to balance quality with price.

Itinerary

Time Management

 From the day you leave until the day you return you'll want to pace your activities carefully. Time management is critical and the more movement you plan between locations each day will not only impact your transportation costs but may contribute to problems navigating traffic to and from each destination in a timely manner.

If your schedule is too hectic it can frustrate your students and chaperones and cause tension within the group. Encourage everyone on the trip to have a watch or cell phone to keep track of time. Schedule your reporting times fifteen minutes earlier than when you actually need to assemble your group. This will help to keep you on your schedule.

Avoid idol downtime in the hotel. Students with idle time will find ways to fill it and things to do which will often result in mischief and trouble. It will be much easier to get your students in their rooms and to bed if you return to the hotel after a well-planned full day of activity.

Transportation

Liability protection and the safety and security of your students should be your number one priority when planning your trip. Getting to your destination and back home again safely will depend upon the choices you make with your travel company regarding charter bus service, and or commercial or charter air carriers. The options are many and the costs vary greatly. Consider the following when making your choices.

Charter Bus Service

- ✓ What's their safety record?
- ✓ Consider the age of their equipment and the frequency of their maintenance schedule?
- ✓ Number of full time vs. part time professional drivers.
- ✓ Can they provide a backup team of fresh drivers for an extended bus trip?
- ✓ Ask for a Certificate of Insurance naming your school district on it.

Commercial Air

- ✓ What's their safety record?
- ✓ Consider the age of their equipment and the frequency of their maintenance schedule?
- ✓ How large of a block of seats can you purchase on each plane?
- ✓ Are your flights direct or connecting?
- ✓ If connecting how long is the layover between flights?

✓ What's their on time flight schedule record?
✓ Are the departure and arrival times similar for all your flights?
✓ What are their luggage restrictions?
✓ Is there an additional luggage fee?
✓ Will they fly your equipment and uniforms?

Charter Air

The cost can vary greatly and will often include a price adjustment clause based upon the cost of jet fuel prior to your departure. Although more expensive per person than commercial airfare there are many advantages to charter service if your budget permits. With charter air service you fly direct, have control over what goes under the plane, and have a more flexible flight schedule and your own departure gate. Check prices with several charter carriers to find equipment that best accommodates the size of your group. If you have extra seats available offer them to school administrators and friends and families of the band to fill out your plane.

Whether flying commercial or charter air prior to your departure check the TSA website (Transportation Safety Administration) for the latest information on security and luggage restrictions. Their link is available in the resources section of this book.

Trucking Your Equipment and Uniforms by Tractor Trailer

Depending upon your travel distance and mode of transportation you may want to consider hiring a trucking company to transport your equipment and uniforms in place of your band trailer. You may be able to find a local trucking company or independent trucker in your community that would be willing to donate their services or discount the cost. If you are flying to your destination I would advise trucking your equipment and uniforms rather than loading them under the plane. Commercial carriers may not be willing to fly your equipment.

Rental Car or Van

In addition to your group transportation have your travel company arrange to have a car or van available for staff and chaperone use while on site to run errands, get to meetings, and handle any emergency situations that may arise.

Hotel

To provide a safe and secure environment for your students choose a hotel wisely. A hotel with outside entrance doors is more difficult to supervise and less secure from strangers. A hotel where the doors open to an inside corridor will facilitate easier supervision and provide less accessibility to outsiders. Avoid a hotel that is located in a questionable neighborhood. Consider the overall condition and cleanliness of the facility as well as the professionalism of the hotel staff.

The layout of the hallways, number of elevators, and configuration of the rooms will affect your ability to monitor your group. Long straight hallways work best. The more elevators there are the easier it will be to handle a large group. In a high rise facility more floors means a much longer wait for the elevators. If other guests will be located on your floors ask the hotel to keep all of your rooms blocked together. Block your male and female student rooms on separate floors. Have the hotel schedule morning wakeup calls, lock or empty the mini fridge and block pay per view movie channels and long distance calls to avoid extra room charges.

Have your students complete a room inspection form identifying any damage they notice upon check-in. Your travel company may provide a form, if not I have included a sample you can use in the resources section of this book. Remind your students that they are responsible for any damage they cause to their room. Collect the forms and keep them on file. Have your chaperones use them when they do the final room inspections before your group checks out of the hotel. This will protect your students from any false damage accusations by the hotel.

Meals

Meals can vary in price dramatically and you'll want to make choices that are healthy, cost effective and appealing to your students. While fast-food meals cost much less they are lacking in quality and substance. You may find it necessary to include a few in your itinerary but for the bulk of your trip make quality meal choices.

Vary your breakfast, lunch and dinner menus each day. Consider incorporating a different theme each night for your dinners such as Italian Night, Mexican Night, or Seafood Night. Your travel representative can check on restaurant seating capacity and make advance reservations for you. If your group is exceptionally large have them arrange to buyout an entire restaurant for several hours and include a special menu with three or four meal options for your students. I've done this on several of my band trips with restaurants like the Hard Rock Cafe, Planet Hollywood, Bubba Gump's, Buca di Beppo's and the Rain Forest Café. If parts of your itinerary are such that providing a group meal is difficult i.e. in a theme park give your students a meal voucher or cash allotment they can use at their leisure.

When making your menu decisions you'll need to account for any students that have special diet requirements and food allergies. Work with your travel representative to provide alternative meal choices for these students. Students with food allergies often carry an EpiPen on them for use in emergency situations. Be sure to advise your chaperones and medical personnel of any students with these issues. A food allergy can often cause a severe reaction that will require immediate medical attention.

Breakfasts are often easier to do in the grand ballroom of your hotel. Although a bit more expensive a breakfast buffet can offer choices that you can vary daily including pancakes, waffles, bagels, eggs, home fries, bacon, sausage, cereal, fruit, milk, orange juice, apple juice, tomato juice, tea and coffee. Since you have a captive audience, breakfast is the perfect time to meet, make announcements, address any overnight issues and give your students their "need to know" information for the day.

While on route to your destination meals can often be time consuming and challenging to manage. If you're bussing pack hoagies, apples, chips, cookies and a drink in the storage bins under the bus for distribution during a roadside rest stop. On longer bus trips divide your busses up between several fast food outlets off the interstate exits to avoid overcrowding and expedite the process or stop at a large mall with a food court.

Set time parameters for all your rest stops and meal stops to make the most efficient use of time while on the road. Before students step off the bus tell them how much time they will have and when they need to be back on the bus. Be consistent and reasonable with your allotted time for each stop and you'll be back on the road again towards your final destination.

Sightseeing

Plan an itinerary that provides the opportunity for your students to visit some of the prominent historic landmarks, national parks, cultural treasures, theme parks or other points of interest near your destination. Balance your choices with opportunities that are cost effective and provide quality educational and entertainment value for your students.

Here are some event, sightseeing, restaurant and attraction suggestions for the places that I traveled with my band.

New York City—Macy's Thanksgiving Day Parade & NYC Nation's Day Parade
- Times Square, Ground Zero, South Street Seaport, Battery Park, Statue of Liberty, Ellis Island, Wall Street, Radio City Music Hall, St. Patrick's Cathedral, Rockefeller Center, 5th Avenue shopping, Medieval Times Dinner Theater, walking tour of lower Manhattan, Statin Island Ferry, Circle One Cruise Line, dinner in Little Italy, Hard Rock Cafe

Chicago—McDonald's Thanksgiving Day Parade
- Navy Pier, Hancock Building Observatory, Medieval Times Dinner Theater, Rainforest Café, Christkindlmarket, walking tour of the city

Philadelphia—Thanksgiving Day Parade
- Liberty Bell, Independence Hall, Spirit of Philadelphia Dinner Cruise, walking tour of the historic district, Old Town Country Buffet

Pasadena—Tournament of Roses Parade
- Hollywood tour day, Santa Monica tour day, LA Farmer's Market, Rose Parade Float Tour, Rose Bowl, Old Town Pasadena, Bubba Gump's, Santa Monica Pier, Disneyland, Universal Studios, City Walk, Six Flags Magic Mountain, Hard Rock Café

Phoenix—Fort McDowell Fiesta Bowl Parade
- Grand Canyon Railroad rails to the rim, Sedona, Old Town Scottsdale, Rawhide, Kiwanis Wave Pool, Organ Stop Pizza Parlor, Montezuma's Castle, Rustler's Rooste, Box Canyon

Orlando—Florida Citrus Parade & Disney Spectro Magic evening parade
- Disney World, Universal, Rain Forest Café, Planet Hollywood, Blue Man Group

Toronto—Santa Claus Parade
- Niagara Falls, CN Tower, Toronto Blue Jays Stadium, Musical Theater, Medieval Times Dinner Theater, Eaton Mall, Hockey Hall of Fame

Louisville—Kentucky Derby Festival Pegasus Parade
- Spirit Dinner Cruise, Louisville Slugger Baseball Factory, Old Country Buffet

Butler Golden Tornado Band at the Navy Pier in Chicago—2011.
Photo by Jeff Groves

Butler Golden Tornado Band dining at Rustler's Rooste in Phoenix, Arizona—2010.
Photo by Jeff Groves

Butler Golden Tornado Band marching in the Chicago
McDonald's Thanksgiving Day Parade—2011.
Photo by Jeff Groves

Religious Obligations

 If your travel plans include a Sunday or overlap a religious celebration, holiday or day of obligation you may need to provide time for those students that are interested to attend religious services. Check with your school district regarding any requirements they may have regarding worship opportunities and student travel plans. Depending upon the religious diversity within your group this may be difficult to accommodate. A viable alternative is to provide time for your students to organize and run a voluntary non-denominational worship opportunity on their own in the hotel ballroom.

Pre-trip Inspection Visit

It's a good idea to schedule an onsite inspection visit months before your trip departure. Use this visit to evaluate facilities and meet with all the vendors and service providers you'll be dealing with on your trip. Visit rehearsal and performance sites and check the driving distance and time required to get to and from the various destinations on your itinerary.

Many events including the Pasadena Tournament of Roses Parade, Macy's Thanksgiving Day Parade, and Fort McDowell Fiesta Bowl Parade require directors to make a pre-trip visit and attend an orientation meeting several months in advance of their event. At the orientation meeting you'll meet parade officials and your band liaison, review policies, procedures, site maps and other pertinent information contained in the band director's handbook.

What Will It Cost?

Cost Per Student

Once you have approved your travel package you can lock in the cost for each student, chaperone and staff member. Most travel companies will provide a number of complimentary packages based upon the number of paying participants. You'll need to decide how to use those packages and how you will handle your staff and chaperones costs. Most directors use the complimentary packages for their staff and spouses and provide a reduced trip plan for the chaperones. Your travel representative can assist you with working out these details and a pricing plan.

To confirm your trip you'll need to sign a contract and pay a non-refundable deposit for each of your participating students. Before you sign a contract check the company's cancellation and refund policy. Your remaining balance will be divided into payments over several months with a final payment due thirty days prior to your departure.

Collecting payments can often be tedious. Some people always procrastinate and pay late. To help avoid late payments structure your due dates at least two weeks in advance of your scheduled payment to your travel company. Some companies offer a direct payment option where parents can make their payments and track their accounts online. If you choose to collect all funds through the band you should purchase bond insurance to protect your organization from loss of funds through any theft or embezzlement. The amount of money collected for a trip can be significant. Limit the number of people that will handle money and list them in your bond insurance policy.

Fundraising

Select a fundraising chairperson to organize a committee and schedule appropriate projects that will coincide with your trip payment schedule. For each project assign a person to organize the sale, provide information to the band families, collect orders, count money, and coordinate help for product distribution and track student sales and profit. A project summary listing individual student profit should then be given to the person in charge of recording all student account information.

You can provide online access to trip account information using an Excel spreadsheet and assigning a four digit ID number to each student. By using an ID number instead of their name they can locate their account and check their trip balance confidentially. It's also a good idea to periodically provide parents with an individual account printout to verify that all funds have been properly accounted for.

Fundraising Ideas

- Product sales—hoagies, pizza, pepperoni rolls, cookie dough, candles, fruit, flowers, magazine subscriptions, frozen food, pies, discount coupon books, discount cards
- Raffles—50/50, Gas Card, Electronics, Automobile, Pro Sport Team Tickets, Theater or concert tickets
- Sponsor and event—Marching Band Shows/Competitions, DCI Show, Concerts, Auctions, Bingo, Carnival, Bake sale, Car wash, Spaghetti dinners, Pancake breakfasts
- Solicit corporate and individual donations
- Apply for grants

Managing Student Accounts

 Accurate accounting and fiscal responsibility are paramount. Obtain a bond insurance policy to cover any individuals that will be handling money. If any of the people named in the bond policy are charged with mishandling funds or theft the organization is protected based on the dollar amount of your bond policy. Check with a local insurance agent for more information. A $50,000 policy should be adequate for most organizations.

Never allow students to handle money and limit the number of adults to a trusted few who are named in your bond policy. Require a minimum of two authorized signatures on all the checks you write and have your financial records audited yearly.

Ask your students to turn in fundraising money and trip payments by check. Cash is harder to track and could easily be misplaced or mishandled. All money should be collected in a sealed envelope identifying what the funds are for i.e. payment, donation or fundraiser and labeled with the students name, grade and section in the band. Never accept a check or cash from a student unless it is in a sealed envelope and properly identified. Maintain a collection box and make it available daily for students to turn in money as needed.

On occasion you may have a few students who are having difficulty making trip payments or participating in fundraising activities due to an extenuating circumstance in the home. This can be an extremely sensitive and embarrassing situation for the student and family and should be handled discreetly in complete confidence. Mom or dad may have just lost their job, gotten a divorce, passed away suddenly or was diagnosed with a terminal illness. Whenever possible try to help these students. Create a fund to assist needy students. Organize a special project i.e. raffle, spaghetti dinner, or look to service clubs in your community or individuals who might be willing to sponsor a student. I was always impressed by the amount of generous people in our community that would call and offer to help students who were having financial problems. Many of them asked to remain anonymous.

Their hardship may be temporary and by providing a loan to cover the trip balance their child can still be a part of the band trip. Each case is unique and should be handled on its own merit. Draw up a loan agreement to be signed by the parent and band director stating the terms and dates for repayment of the trip money. If the funds are not repaid according to the terms of the agreement turn the balance due in as a school obligation. When a student has an obligation on file the school will withhold grades and in the case of a senior their diploma until the obligation is satisfied in full. A sample agreement form is provided in the resources section of this book.

Family & Friends Trip

A family & friends trip is a great way to provide interested parents, relatives and friends with an opportunity to support the band, see their performance and share in their student's trip experience. Have your travel company create a trip package that is similar to the bands and include a few common itinerary items where students and parents can spend time together. A day at a theme park or sightseeing attraction i.e. Niagara Falls, the Grand Canyon, Navy Pier, Broadway show or a dinner theater event such as Medieval Times work well.

To avoid any interference, unnecessary or unwanted parent contact during the trip it's best to keep transportation and housing separate from that of the band. All correspondence, reservations and payments related to the Family & Friends trip should be handled directly with the travel company and not through the band.

Butler Golden Tornado Band students and families spend time together
at the Medieval Times Dinner Theater in Chicago—2011.
Photo by Jeff Groves

Safety & Security

An ounce of prevention is worth a pound of cure! Turn on the evening news and you'll hear about a terrorist bombing, child abduction or shooting at a school, mall or movie theater. Today more than ever you must be diligent and examine all facets of your travel plan with a greater emphasis on student safety and security. I was always traveling with fourteen through eighteen year old students. My rules, guidelines, curfews and methods of supervision were fairly strict to assure parents and administrators that the students would be monitored very closely while on the trip. If you're traveling with a younger group age thirteen and under much stricter rules, curfews, and methods of supervision are essential. When traveling with college students you can be a bit more relaxed.

Safe Travel Dos & Don'ts

- Travel with additional school personnel whenever possible.
- Before departure leave a file in your school office that includes student lists, bus and or flight assignments, parent phone numbers, transportation carriers, travel company emergency contacts, rooming lists, staff list, chaperone list, itinerary, and other important contact numbers in the event of an emergency.
- Program the phone numbers of your principal and superintendent in your cell phone and call them immediately in the event of any emergency situation.
- In advance of your trip provide students and parents with a copy of trip rules, discipline guidelines and behavior expectations as well as the procedure you will follow for dealing with any infractions that may occur.
- Label all luggage, uniform garment bags and instrument cases.
- Provide parents back home with emergency contact information and numbers.
- Take an adequate number of chaperones to supervise your group.
- Require all adults that will travel with your group to obtain proper child abuse and criminal background clearances as required in your state. Keep their clearances on file with your school.
- Adults that will travel with your group must follow the same school student guidelines regarding the use and possession of weapons, alcohol, drugs and tobacco products.
- Adults must refrain from consuming alcoholic beverages during the entire trip.
- Adults should refrain from smoking in the presence of students.
- Emergency medical forms with an attached student photo should be organized alphabetically in binders by bus and available at all times.
- Bring a reasonable amount of emergency cash along on the trip.
- Students must complete a luggage & carry-on bag parent verification form or have their luggage inspected by a teacher and adult witness before departure.

- Students must stay in groups of four or more when off the bus or away from the hotel complex.
- Students must wear matching band attire i.e. varsity jacket, windbreaker, or T-shirt when off the bus or away from the hotel complex.
- Students are not permitted to leave the group hotel or depart from the itinerary to go with visiting relatives.
- Use two way radios and cell phones to keep adults in constant communication. Create a cell phone list with the names and numbers of all the adults on the trip and program them on your phone before departure.
- Always travel with medical personnel i.e. a registered nurse, EMT, or certified paramedic.
- Prepare a medical bag and have it available throughout the trip.
- Choose a hotel in a safe neighborhood with inside access doors and straight hallways.
- Have your hotel block long distance calls, pay per view television and either lock or empty the mini fridge to avoid students incurring additional room costs.
- Block your male and female rooms on separate floors.
- Locate chaperone rooms on each floor near the stairwell and in the middle of the hall near the elevators.
- Don't place any signs or tape across student doorways.
- Conduct a room check nightly to verify students are in their assigned rooms at curfew.
- In addition to hotel security hire a private security firm to monitor your hallways overnight.

Overnight Hotel Security

Most hotels have security personnel and video cameras that monitor hallway and exit door activity 24/7. Hotel security personnel will make their rounds at periodic intervals during the night checking all the floors. They will not exclusively stay on your floors to monitor your rooms. Have your travel company arrange for a private security firm to oversee the floors your students are assigned to. Each morning you'll receive a written report sighting any incident that had occurred overnight and the action taken to resolve the situation.

Refrain from placing student's names on doors and taping doorways. This sends a clear signal to other guests that these rooms are occupied with students.

School District Liability Release Forms

Most school districts require a release of liability form for groups scheduling overnight travel. While they encourage student travel and accept it as a viable part of a child's education they don't want to be held liable if something goes wrong. Your travel company can provide liability insurance to protect you and your students.

Chaperones

An adequate and knowledgeable team of chaperones is essential. Insist that they obtain the same child abuse and criminal background clearances that are required to be a teacher in your state. Since I was traveling with a mixed group I preferred to use husband and wife chaperone teams. Follow your school district guideline for their required chaperone to student ratio. If your district doesn't have a policy I would recommend a ratio of one adult for every fifteen students.

We all parent differently. Some of us tolerate behavior that others wouldn't. Your chaperones should be mentored and given guidance on how you expect them to supervise the students. When situations arise that require implementation of school rules or policy they should be handled by the band director or other school employee.

Chaperones should be familiar with the students that are assigned to their bus and have access to information regarding those with special medical needs or issues i.e. asthma, food or bee sting allergies, allergies to certain medications or students that are diabetic or subject to seizures.

Every band has a few students that "walk to the beat of a different drummer" so to speak. Most directors have a pretty good handle on those with unique personalities or behavioral quirks and sharing this information with your chaperones can give them a better perspective on how to deal with these individuals.

Each year when you add chaperones, assign a new couple with a veteran couple who can serve as their mentors for the band season. Remind all of your chaperones that they should never use profanity or touch a student under any circumstance. A touch may be misconstrued as inappropriate attention and lead to accusations against that adult. The only acceptable situation where it's okay to touch a student would be when helping during a medical emergency i.e. fainting, choking, epileptic seizure, stabilizing a broken bone or stopping severe bleeding.

Always use the same chaperones with the same group of students for your entire band season. Consistency is the key to successful supervision. When most problems occur they can be traced back to miscommunication or a total lack of communication. When the chaperones on one bus give different instructions to their students than the chaperones on all the other busses you have a problem. Make sure every student receives the same information, in the same way, at the same time. Schedule a brief morning or evening meeting to keep your staff and chaperones on the same page.

Medical Personnel

In addition to chaperones you should always travel with a certified nurse, EMT, or paramedic. If you have a large group one person is not sufficient. You may need as many as three or four nurses to adequately take care of your group. Having several nurses on your trip will give you the flexibility to setup a rotating schedule so the same person is not always on duty each evening.

Keep a medical bag or a first aid kit with you at all times when you are out and about sightseeing with your group. Make sure your chaperones have the binder with the medical emergency release forms for their bus with them at all times. Each evening the nurses should collect all binders and have them available throughout the night in the event there's an emergency and a student needs to be transported to the hospital.

The band director should be informed of all medical situations immediately and whenever possible should go to the hospital with the nurse and the sick or injured student. Parents should be notified as soon as possible and kept informed of their child's condition. Depending on the severity of the situation you should call your principal and superintendent and keep them apprised of the student's condition. If circumstances are such that the student needs to return home your travel company can assist you in making the necessary arrangements.

Whether your school provides a nurse or you recruit a volunteer nurse, EMT or paramedic from your band parents or community, including a medical professional should always be a vital part of your overall safety plan.

Medical Forms

You must keep accurate medical release forms on hand at all times when traveling. I used a two sided form which I've included in the resources section of this book. Side one was modeled after our school districts standard field trip medical release form. It covers the legalities involved when authorizing emergency medical treatment in the absence of a parent or guardian and includes parent insurance carrier and policy number information. Side two was created by one of my band nurses who had worked in a hospital emergency room and documents the student's medical history. This form came in handy on numerous occasions while traveling with the band over the years.

On the advice of a band parent who was a Pennsylvania State Trooper we decided to attach a color photo of each student to the upper right hand corner of their medical form. A photo can be sent electronically to multiple law enforcement agencies to aid in the search for a missing person. I never had to use that photo but it was good to know it was there if I ever did.

Many parades require marching members to carry a copy of their medical release form under their uniform in the event they need medical assistance during the parade. Forms can be duplicated folded and placed in a small plastic pouch attached to a lanyard and worn under their uniform.

Dealing with Sick Students

During one of my first trips I had a student come down with the flu bug and it quickly spread throughout the band. If I could have isolated that student early on it might have minimized the problem. After that experience I always reserved two extra hotel rooms to use as sick rooms. One room would be used

for male students and the other for female students that became ill and had to be isolated from their roommates. A few hotels were gracious and didn't charge for the sick rooms if we didn't use them during our stay.

Student Supervision

If your students all have the same band windbreaker, varsity jacket, or T-shirt choose the one that would be best suited for the climate you're traveling to. Require all students to wear that attire whenever they are off the busses or out of the hotel complex. It's much easier to supervise a group when they all look alike. Your students will obviously stand out in a crowd and that will often prompt people to stop and ask, what's with the matching jackets. My band enjoyed all the special attention they received and were eager to answer all the questions. What group are you with? Where are you from? How big is the group? Are you performing in the parade? What an honor! Good luck, we'll be cheering for you!

Whenever you're giving your students some time to explore an area on their own i.e. Times Square, give them parameters (*stay within 2 blocks in either direction*) and time limits (*2 hours*) and designate an appropriate area to assemble when time is up (*check-in with your chaperones in the center island near the bleacher seats*). Before you excuse your students reinforce the importance of staying in groups, looking out for each other and guarding their wallets and purses. Remind them to be courteous, watch their language and avoid overt displays of public affection.

When meeting your students have chaperones spread apart in the designated assembly location and hold lamented numbered bus signs. Conduct a quick head count and if numbers don't agree call roll to see who's missing from the group. When a student or group of students fail to return on time give them a few extra minutes before assigning two adults to begin looking for them. If they are not located within a reasonable amount of time contact the police for their assistance.

Handling Discipline Problems

Unfortunately you may have to deal with an unpleasant situation involving a student or group of students that make a poor decision while on the trip. It may involve the use of alcohol, drugs, or tobacco products, shop lifting, hotel damage, bullying or sexual misconduct. It's important that you have clearly defined rules and policies in place to help address these types of problems. Refer to your schools student handbook for guidance.

Notify the proper school official and the parents of each student who are involved immediately. Discuss with your principal the appropriate measures and discipline you should enforce and what actions will be taken when the student returns home. Based upon the severity of the incident you may decide to send the student home at the parent's expense.

Luggage & Carry-on Bag Check—Parent Verification Form

I created a luggage & carry-on bag check form to place the responsibility for inspecting a student's luggage squarely with their parents. There is no easy way to adequately check several hundred pieces of luggage in a timely manner on the day of your departure. This form resolves that problem and provided a way to guard against students bringing contraband items on the trip.

The form verifies that parents have carefully checked their child's luggage and confirm that it doesn't contain any weapons, controlled substances i.e. drugs, alcohol or tobacco products. By signing this form a parent understands that if their child is caught with any of these items they will be removed from the trip and sent home at the parent's expense. In addition school district rules and regulations will be enforced and may result in a suspension and or expulsion from both the band and school.

Any student that shows up on the day of departure without a signed form will need to have their luggage inspected by a school employee and an adult witness to be allowed to go on the trip.

Uniforms & Equipment

Packing and Transporting Your Uniforms & Equipment

Have you ever watched an airline load luggage? Flying your performance equipment and uniforms with a commercial or charter airline can be a risky venture. Everything must be packed carefully and you'll need to know the weight and dimensions of each item. Commercial carriers may refuse to fly these items or charge an excessive amount to transport them.

When flying to your destination it's much easier to truck your equipment and uniforms. Instead of asking a band dad to tow your equipment trailer across the country hire a trucking company with a 48' or 53' trailer to transport all of your equipment and uniforms. When you hire a trucking company you can control the packing, proper loading and unloading of all your items. Check around in your area you may be able to find a local independent trucker or trucking company that will donate their time and equipment or offer a significant discount to help you out. You may even have a parent who is in the trucking business.

Pack your uniforms in standard garment boxes which are available from most moving and trucking companies. You can usually fit ten band uniforms in their garment bag in each box. Pack the uniforms in alphabetical order and then number each box to help with onsite setup and organization. Give each student the number for the box their uniform is located in. On the outside of each box indicate the student's last name for the first and last uniform in the alphabetical sequence i.e. Box #1 Adams thru Barker.

Your school district should have the necessary insurance rider available to protect your equipment and uniforms and the carrier should also have insurance to protection you. Create a detailed manifest naming all of the items you'll be transporting and give one copy to the driver, one to your school district business office and keep a copy for your records. Take cell phone pictures of the inside of the truck to record how it was loaded and secured.

Meetings

Trip Presentation Meeting

Once you have the all your trip details schedule a parent meeting to share your plan, present the itinerary, outline the cost, and list fundraising opportunities and review your system for tracking student accounts. If possible have a representative from your travel company make a presentation on the trip package followed by a question and answer period.

Schedule a separate meeting for the band to share the itinerary as well as performance aspects of their trip. Schedule a final parent meeting one week before departure and a final student meeting after your last rehearsal.

Final Parent Trip Meeting

Schedule a mandatory parent trip meeting one week before departure and review the following items.

- ✓ Changes in medical insurance provider information
- ✓ Changes in medical history
- ✓ Medical emergencies and contact information
- ✓ Dealing with students that become ill on the trip
- ✓ Students that must travel with prescription drugs
- ✓ Discipline guidelines and procedure for handling problems
- ✓ Methods of transportation
- ✓ Damage to Hotel property
- ✓ Trip Itinerary
- ✓ Packing Guidelines
- ✓ Requests for alternate transportation to and or from the trip destination.

Final Student Trip Meeting

Schedule a trip meeting for the band after your last rehearsal. Invite your principal to address the band, acknowledge their accomplishments and reinforce the fact that all school rules and policies will apply on the trip. Distribute and review all your trip handouts paying special attention to the trip guidelines outlined below.

- ☐ Departure day, date and student reporting time.
- ☐ Parking instructions for leaving a vehicle on school property during the trip.

- [ ] When you arrive at the school report to the auditorium, find the location for your assigned bus and report to that area with your luggage.
- [ ] Check in with your chaperones.
- [ ] Wear comfortable casual clothes for travel such as blue jeans, a sweatshirt or sweater, comfortable shoes and socks and the band windbreaker.
- [ ] Snack foods may be packed in your carry-on bag any bottled drink must be in a clear sealed plastic container.
- [ ] You're responsible for carrying and loading luggage (carry-on bag and suitcase) throughout the duration of the trip.
- [ ] You must wear the band windbreaker to aid in group supervision when off the bus.
- [ ] School district rules & policies apply throughout the trip.
- [ ] You are expected to follow instructions from the band staff, chaperones, bus drivers, travel company representatives, and hotel staff. Disrespect will not be tolerated.
- [ ] PDA—overt public display of affection is inappropriate and school policy will apply.
- [ ] Only the roommates assigned to a room are permitted in that room and on that floor—under no circumstance should guys be in girl's rooms or floors or vice versa. There are numerous public places at the hotel where you and your friends can gather and visit.
- [ ] Students are not permitted to leave the hotel with visiting relatives.
- [ ] Students must adhere to all hotel policies & rules / there are video cameras throughout the hotel for your protection. Security guards will be on duty on each floor overnight.
- [ ] Students must follow all scheduled evening curfew times.
- [ ] Each evening a different nurse will be on duty if need medical assistance.
- [ ] Damage to your hotel room will be assessed to your parents.
- [ ] Students must stay in groups of 4 or more when we are out and about.
- [ ] If you become a discipline problem you'll be sent home at your parent's expense.
- [ ] Our hotel is a great facility—treat it with respect—there will be other guests in the hotel with us and I expect you to respect their privacy and watch noise levels—they paid a lot more than you did to stay at this hotel.
- [ ] You must be quiet, respectful and listen carefully to anyone that is giving you information or instructions on this trip
- [ ] On performance day you must wear your medical lanyard under your uniform.
- [ ] Be on time or early for all bus departures and meetings.
- [ ] Report any issues with your hotel room immediately.

If you're flying to your destination arrange for a pilot to come in and speak to your students. You'll probably have a few seasoned flyers in the group but the majority of your students will more than likely be first time flyers and some may be afraid to fly. Ask the pilot to speak on the following topics in his presentation and follow up with a question and answer session: airport security, boarding passes, boarding the plane, seating assignments, carry-on storage, preflight preparations, preflight instructions, backing away from the terminal, preparation for takeoff, takeoff, landing gear noises, climbing to altitude, cabin pressure and inner ear pressure adjustments, slow descent, inner ear pressure adjustments, final preparation for landing, landing gear noises, landing, arrival at the terminal, disembarking the plane and luggage claim.

Chaperone Trip Meeting

Two weeks before your trip schedule a dinner meeting to thank you chaperones for all they do and to discuss the upcoming trip in detail and give them their trip information packet. After the meal use a power point presentation to go through the itinerary in detail including pictures from your pre-trip inspection tour. Cover every aspect of the trip including bus lists and assignments, roll call, specific chaperone duties, hotel supervision, rehearsal day, performance day, medical concerns, breakfast meetings and methods of communication during the trip. After your presentation allow time for answering questions. Your chaperones will now have a few weeks to read over the material in preparation for the trip.

Public Relations—Promoting Your Trip

Once you've finalized your plans, received approval, and met with your parents it's time to get the word out to the public. If you don't promote your program no one else will. Send out a press release to your local newspapers and radio and television stations to spread the good news about your trip and performance. Sharing your story with the community will give your students a sense of pride and accomplishment and reinforce the positive things going on in your school.

In most schools the most visible part of the Music Department is the marching band. Whether that's right or wrong having a strong marching band will reflect positively on the community's perception of your entire Music program.

Organizing Your Students

Room Assignments

Arbitrarily assigning students as roommates is easier but can often result in compatibility issues that cause tension and problems within the room. Instead allow your students to choose their roommates. Quad occupancy is the norm for student travel however your numbers may not always divide perfectly by four. Give senior students the first opportunity to fill any rooms of two, or three that you'll need to balance things out. Handle this discreetly and before all other students make their selections. This way you'll know that all of the remaining housing forms must have four names on them when submitted.

Prep your students to begin thinking about their choices well in advance of the day that you'll need that information. Periodically remind them that they must have four students in their room. On the day you're completing forms have each group select a room captain to fill out and submit their rooming list. While on the trip room captains will be issued the key cards and are responsible for turning in a damage report for their room. All lists with less than four names on them should be discarded and those students reorganized in new groups of four.

A sample housing form and hotel check-in damage form are included in the resources section of this book.

Bus and Plane Assignments

Once you have your rooming list you can create your bus and plane assignments. Always keep roommates together on the same bus and plane. Whenever possible keep students on the same bus they rode during football season with the same chaperone team. Make your assignments by seniority starting with the senior class and ending with the freshman.

Packing Guidelines

Most students will need guidance when it comes to packing for the trip. I have included two sample packing checklists in the resources section of this book. One for overnight bus trips and one for trips involving air travel. The lists include essentials as well as optional items. Make sure your students label everything and refrain from bringing unnecessary items. If your students will have an opportunity to purchase souvenirs on the trip advise them to leave some extra room in their suitcase when packing.

If you're flying to your destination visit the TSA website (Transportation Safety Administration) and check with your airlines for specific restrictions on luggage size, carryon bags and packing restrictions.

The Performance

Preparing For Your Performance

Develop a long range rehearsal strategy to prepare your students for their performance. In addition to your normal fall rehearsal schedule and standard appearances at things like football games, band competitions or exhibitions and local parades you may need to prepare additional new music selections, create special routines or learn a new drill.

You may need to extend your marching season through the New Year. If you're marching in the Tournament of Roses or Macy's Thanksgiving Day Parade you'll have additional challenges to prepare for.

Most events will provide a Band Directors Handbook including television script forms, music copyright requirements and restrictions, performance guidelines, reporting times, bus and equipment vehicle passes, maps of the parade route, diagrams of the drop-off and dispersal areas, restroom locations, television camera area and first aid stations. Many will hold a mandatory meeting the day or evening before the event to review procedures and cover any last minute instructions.

Spectator and participant safety and security are a concern for all major events today. Most are monitored by the Department of Homeland Security and have measures in place to deal with the threat of terrorism. Make sure you understand what's in place and how your students should respond during the parade in the event of an incident. Take time to address these items with your staff, students and chaperones.

Band members should have a copy of their medical release form on them while in uniform. A lanyard with a small plastic pouch attached can hold a folded medical release and be worn under the uniform coat or top.

Some events limit the number of chaperones and staff that may go down the parade route with your band. Adults accompanying the band should maintain a professional appearance wearing matching apparel that identifies them as part of your band. In the event of warm weather and a lengthy parade route make sure chaperones carry water bottles or have access to water along the parade route. Many parades will provide water stations along the way. Monitor your band and have a process in place to distribute water to students as needed. Hydration is important especially during a long march.

If you have chaperones follow the band it should be their responsibility to stay with any student that needs to exit the parade due to illness. Using chaperone couples enables you to have a guy to carry the sick student's instrument (this is extremely helpful when the student plays the drums or sousaphone) while the woman attends to the student. Some parades will have officials in golf carts monitoring the route to offer assistance and transport sick students to a medical tent.

Select your music carefully. Some events may have a theme and require a specific genre of music. Whatever the circumstance be sure to choose music that is upbeat, entertaining and arranged to make your band sound its best. Since you will want to play often make sure you consider the range and stamina that will be required to perform your selection. Most of all select music your students will enjoy performing and the audience will enjoy listening to!

Be careful to pace your band and play as often as possible while avoiding extended periods of drum cadence. Since you will have a new audience every block it is not necessary to perform a different selection throughout the entire parade route. In some situations due to music copyright and television restrictions you may need to prepare a separate selection that will only be performed in front of the television cameras. Make sure you know where television coverage begins and ends and play throughout the entire area. If your selection is short be prepared to immediately go into a roll-off and repeat your selection. Most television networks will cut away from your group if you're not playing.

Consider adding simple horn movements to enhance your overall presentation and general effect. Work on refining details such as basic instrument posture and hold. Choose auxiliary unit props and flags for maximize effect and impact.

If the parade, festival or competition you are attending is a judged event make sure you are familiar with the evaluation system and sheets that will be used well in advance and prepare your students accordingly.

Based upon the size of your band and auxiliary unit(s) give careful consideration to how you place instruments and auxiliary members in your parade block formation. Every band is different and what works for one may not for another. Create a band block that will place your best performers on the camera side of the formation. Smaller bands should be careful not to over spread distance and interval in an attempt to look larger. This often results in poor sound projection and exposes marching errors. Strive to achieve maximum impact from your band not only for those along the parade route but your television audience. Keep musicians closer together, arrange your instrumentation to create a balanced wall of sound. Utilize your auxiliary units to create impact and enhance your general effect.

Consider the way your band will sound on television. A microphone location can often pickup an individual player as they march by so proper placement of your strongest musicians is paramount. Think or your arrangement and how it is scored so you can set your instrumentation to provide the best overall balance and blend for your band.

Know your strengths both musically and visually. Play up those elements and hide your weaknesses. I have included a sample parade block diagram in the resources section of this book

Macy's Thanksgiving Day Parade

The Macy's Thanksgiving Day Parade requires each band to create a special routine which is televised nationally near the end of the parade route on 34th Street in front of the Macy's store. You cannot perform the same music which will be televised on NBC at Macy's anywhere else along the parade route. Since several other networks have coverage along the route prepare an additional selection for use until you reach the 34th Street broadcast area.

In October (usually Columbus Day weekend) you'll need to travel to New York with a DVD of your routine to meet with the Macy's parade officials and review your performance plans with NBC. They will either approve your routine as is or suggest changes that you'll need to make for approval of your routine. When your changes are made you will need to submit a new DVD to NBC to get their final approval.

On Thanksgiving morning each band is scheduled by their order of appearance in the parade to rehearse in front of Macy's with the NBC television crew beginning at 3 AM. After your rehearsal you will not be able to leave Manhattan due to the large amount of traffic coming into the city that morning. Arrange to have a breakfast in midtown Manhattan before you bus to Central Park where the parade forms. Keep your students on the coaches until your designated unloading and lineup time.

Check the weather forecast days in advance of your departure to make sure your students bring appropriate attire to wear under their uniform. The weather can vary greatly from a temperature in the high 60's to freezing cold. You might have bright blue skies or it could be overcast with rain, sleet or snow. No matter what, the show goes on! So dress accordingly.

The parade route is a little more than two miles long and packed with people ten to fifteen rows deep along the way. Prepare your students to play a lot with not more than one cadence between selections unless you're marking time in one spot for a prolonged period.

Only a small handful of chaperones are permitted behind the band and they must be dressed in matching attire which identifies them as part of your band. Directors, additional staff and chaperones are not permitted to march through the television area on 34th Street.

The area two blocks before your NBC presentation is designated as the "Quite Zone" created to avoid any bleed over of sound with your group and the group on television. You will stop all playing and literally walk in formation through this area. At the end of the "Quiet Zone" is a red line marking the entrance for your televised performance and when you reach that you can reset your form.

When it's your turn to perform an NBC representative will cue your band to begin and you must be ready to move immediately. As you proceed through the television area you will be able to hear the television commentators talking about your band over a public address system.
Tell your students to ignore the announcements and stay focus on their performance. After your routine you must exit the television area quickly to a holiday selection. You are now only about a block from the end of the parade and the disbursal area. You can expect a tired but elated bunch of kids reflecting on their once in a lifetime accomplishment!

Butler Golden Tornado Band in the Macy's Thanksgiving Day Parade—2002.
Photo by Group Photos.com

Butler Golden Tornado Band performing in Herald Square—2002.
Photo by Group Photos.com

Pasadena Tournament of Roses Parade

The Pasadena Tournament of Roses has the longest parade route of any major event stretching over five and one-half miles. It is imperative that you plan a rehearsal schedule to build both your students physical stamina and playing stamina. The good news is that all major television networks (including global television) are located at the beginning of the parade route. In the middle of the television area is a challenging 105 degree right turn. Throughout this area there are bleacher seats on both sides of the street and all television cameras are located on the right side above the bleachers which are 80 rows high. This area is quite impressive and can be somewhat overwhelming. There are cameras and spotlights everywhere and the crowd reaction to each band is both loud and enthusiastic. As you leave the television area the parade route takes a slight downward dip and then levels out for the rest of the march.

Crowds line the entire five and one-half mile route sometimes as many as 15 rows deep with people sitting on the curb, in chairs, standing and even on ladders wanting to catch a glimpse of the parade. You will want to play often in fact in the television area I had my band play back to back to back to back selections with only a roll-off in between. We played a total of 58 different times during the entire parade route.

The weather is usually warm for this event and it has only rained a handful of times in the history of the Tournament of Roses. Your students must be conditioned to physically meet the demands of this event and the long march. For a reference point the Pasadena City College marks the halfway point in the parade. To give my students a better perspective of the parade route I had our busses drive the parade route a day before the parade.

In order to prepare start in band camp and gradually build up both physical and playing stamina in your daily rehearsals. Include weight lifting to build upper body strength and exercising to help work cardio. At each practice increase the distance your band can comfortably march and play until they can march for five and one-half miles without struggling. One week before your departure test your students with a simulated performance marching and playing for a total of six miles. If they successfully accomplish that feat it will give them the confidence they need to excel in Pasadena. At the end of the parade everyone is treated to a free meal from In & Out Burger. Your students will get a chance to meet and exchange parade pins (parade pins are a big thing—check into getting them for your students) while they enjoy their food at Victory Park.

The tournament is the best at providing information to help you prepare for this event. You will get a band directors handbook and be assigned a direct liaison from the Tournament Committee who will assist you throughout the year. Each band will get a visit from the President of the Tournament of Roses (which you can schedule) to promote your participation and assist you in any way possible in preparing for the event.

Another feature of the Tournament is the Band Fest where bands get to perform their halftime show in front of enthusiastic audiences a few days before the parade. This is a non-competitive band festival designed to showcase your students. The day before the parade the Tournament will hold a meeting for directors and drum majors to go over every facet of the event in detail. There is also a wonderful luncheon gathering at the Ritz Carlton to honor all participating band directors and present parade mementos.

All in all nobody does it better than the Tournament of Roses. They will treat you like gold and your students will be seen on a global stage on the most watched and prestigious parade in the world. In my opinion performing in the Tournament of Roses Parade is like a football team playing in the "Super Bowl". It's the premiere performance opportunity for any band and band director and I'm thankful that I have the chance to experience it twice.

Managing Your Trip

Departure Day

On the day of departure ask your students to report one hour before your scheduled pullout time. Have them assemble in the school auditorium and sit in sections by the bus they're assigned to ride on. Have the chaperones call the roll and report any absentees. Hold a brief meeting to review any last minute instructions and information and to set a positive tone for your trip.

Using Student Volunteers

Whether you already have leadership positions in place or you ask for volunteers there are many ways your students can be of help on your trip. Assign them to assist with loading and unloading luggage, equipment and uniforms and cleaning the inside of the bus at the end of each day. Reward these students with a few special privileges during the trip to thank them for their help.

Loading & Boarding the Busses

Have your male chaperones oversee your student volunteers and carefully place all the luggage in one bin, uniforms in another and miscellaneous item in the third. If you're bussing to an airport to fly to your destination you'll only be loading luggage under each bus. Place any other items you may need access to while on the road where they can be easily reached. Stagger the boarding of the busses one bus at a time once all chaperones are in place and everything is loaded.

On The Road

Bring along several age appropriate DVD's to help pass the time during long bus rides. When traveling with a mixed group of varying ages be careful what you choose to show. Most schools have a policy covering the appropriate use of DVD's in a classroom based upon the movie industries rating system. To be safe you should also adhere to their guidelines when choosing what to show.

For those exceptionally long bus rides try playing a game of movie trivia. After viewing a DVD ask specific question about the movie and award small cash prizes to students with the correct answers. When students have the opportunity to earn some extra cash to spend on the trip they will pay greater attention to the movie. Have your band boosters bring along some extra cash to use for this purpose.

Students that choose to bring electronic devices for listening to their own music or playing games on should always use headphones so they don't disturb others around them. Give your staff and chaperone two seats for themselves in the front of the bus so they can stretch out and relax better.

Rest Stops

Department of Transportation regulations require bus drivers to stop every few hours. A great deal of valuable time can be lost at a rest stop. If given the opportunity students will seek out vending machines and snack food stands. It is important to make it clear to your student's when a stop is a restroom only stop. Tell them to get off the bus quickly and back on again as soon as possible. Station chaperones near the food areas and vending machines. Remind your students that a trip is about the destination not spending hours along the interstate at a rest stop.

To eliminate the use of vending machines while at rest stops have your boosters purchase water, juice boxes, or soda, apples, chips, cookies, or candy to bring on the trip and provide for the students. These items can be packed in coolers and stored in the bins under the bus for easy access.

Hotel Check-in

Keep students on the bus and have a chaperone distribute the key cards to the room captains while your male chaperones and student volunteers unload the luggage from underneath. Once luggage is off the bus and lined up neatly in rows excuse the students to find their luggage and go to their rooms.

Have all room captains complete a room damage report. Your travel company may have a form for this if not I have included a sample form in the resources section of this book. Keep these forms together and make them available when your chaperones do their final room checks. If any damage is discovered that was not listed on the report notify the parents of those students and let them know they will be responsible to make restitution.

Organizing Your Uniforms & Equipment in the Hotel

Have your travel representative arrange for the hotel to provide a room that you can lock to organize and store your equipment and uniforms in. It's best to keep all these items out of the student rooms.

Transporting uniforms in garment boxes is a great way to keep them neat and organized. Available through moving companies you can usually fit ten uniforms in their garment bags in each box. Pack your uniforms in alphabetical order and number each box to aid in arranging them at your hotel. For ease of distribution and collection give your students the number of the box their uniform is located in. Line all of your instruments up by like kind and section in the same room to keep everything you'll need for rehearsal and your performance together in one place.

Pack extra uniform items i.e. shoes, plumes, gloves and even a complete uniform or two along with drumsticks and drumheads, extra auxiliary props, flags, poles and pompoms. Bring duct tape, electrical ties, packing tape, some tools and an instrument repair kit. Include a sewing kit with extra uniform buttons and a needle and thread for making emergency repairs.

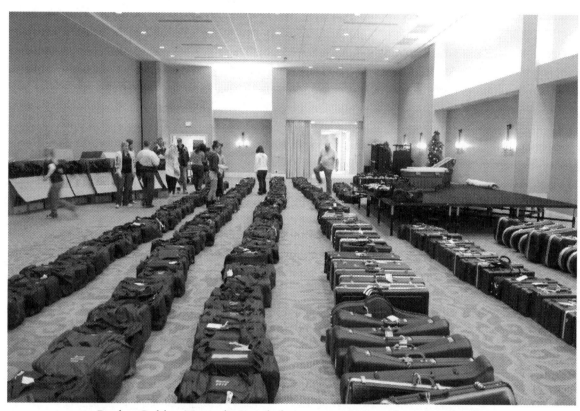

Butler Golden Tornado Band chaperones and staff organizing the
uniforms and equipment in our hotel—Fiesta Bowl Trip 2010.
Photo by Jeff Groves

Overnight Hotel Supervision

When you plan your trip give your travel representative specific instructions on how you would like your student, chaperone, staff and medical personnel rooms blocked in the hotel. If you're staying in a multilevel hotel male and female rooms should always be on separate floors and chaperone rooms near the middle or ends of the hallway. Block the rooms for your medical personnel and sick rooms together and locate them on the same floor as your female students near the elevators. Block all your staff rooms together on a separate floor away from the student rooms.

If your hotel is all on one level with front and back exits it will present a challenge for chaperones to monitor as well as an increased security risk from outsiders. Hire a private security company to remain outside and monitor your block of rooms overnight. The only benefit this kind of facility provides is that it is easier for students get to and from their rooms quickly when leaving your hotel for scheduled events. In the same sense it's also much easier for them to sneak out of their room which is a problem.

Make sure your students know how to get medical help if they become ill during the night. Give the phone extension and room number for the evening on-duty nurse to your chaperones so they can inform the students as they make their evening room checks. Instruct your chaperones and overnight security guards to notify you of any problems or medical issues that occur during the night.

Refrain from placing signs on doors and taping doorways on student rooms at night. This only signals other hotel guests that those rooms are occupied by students. Give your chaperones and staff a complete rooming list with names and room numbers for all of your students.

Divide the total number of rooms on each floor into smaller groups and assign each chaperone couple to a group they'll be responsible for while in the hotel. At evening curfew they should begin the room checks for their assigned group. To insure that all students are in their assigned room knock on the door and ask to see each of them. Do not enter their room instead ask them to come to the door. If all students are present and accounted for give them the nurse information and the times for lights out, their morning wakeup call and breakfast.

Most hotels have security cameras on each floor that monitor the hallways and exits and security personnel who will periodically do rounds to check the floors overnight. Schedule your own private security guards to be on duty from your evening curfew to your morning wakeup call. Each morning you will receive a written summary of any incidents that occurred overnight and the actions they took to resolve them.

Morning Meetings

Schedule your breakfasts in the hotel ballroom and use this opportunity to meet with your group each morning. Once everyone has finished eating get their attention, greet your students and begin your talk with some positive comments. I want to thank you for being so cooperative yesterday when we checked into the hotel, or the manager of the Hard Rock Café told me you were the most well-mannered group of students he has ever had in his restaurant, kudos. Think of something you can use each day to start your meeting on a lighter note. If you're at a loss tell a music joke they're always good for a groan from the band!

Address any concerns or issues next. If there are none give your students their "need to know" information for the day. Save the specifics for your staff and chaperones the students won't remember them anyhow. Excuse the students to go up to their rooms and get the things they'll need for the day while you meet briefly with your staff and chaperones. Refer to the packet of trip information you gave them and make sure everyone is up to speed on the specific plans for the day.

Dealing with Adversity

No matter how much planning goes into a trip even the best laid plans can be disrupted by the unforeseen. Learn to expect the unexpected when traveling. Always have a "Plan B". Your travel company can provide that safety net or "Plan B" for most of the problems you might encounter while on your trip. It may be a sudden weather event, bus breakdown or accident, flight cancellation or delay, or a medical emergency. You might have to extend your stay an additional day or two. Whatever the situation they have the experience, knowledge and resources at their fingertips to get you through the rough times. That's why you hired them.

If a problem does arise no matter how concerned and frustrated you are by the circumstances always remain calm. The way you handle these situations and the image you project will influence those around you. A positive attitude can be contagious.

There is one aspect of your trip that your travel company won't be able to resolve with a "Plan B" for you and that's your performance. You're the expert when it comes to this part of the trip. We all know some pretty crazy things can happen during a performance. Do some brainstorming with your students during rehearsals and talk about some "what if" scenarios and possible solutions. For example, what if the percussion section misses the roll-off signal when you enter the television area? What if part of the band gets out of sync with the rest of the group? What if the camera crew gets in your way? You could go on and on. If your band is well rehearsed chances are none of these things will ever happen. The key to success is preparation! Practice, practice, practice!

Onsite Rehearsal

You will need an adequate rehearsal facility while on your trip. When you plan your itinerary make sure you include an appropriate block of time for rehearsal. Let your travel representative know if you will need separate places for music and marching rehearsal, a paved surface to practice parade marching or a lined football field. Make sure there are restrooms and water available at the site. Have a backup indoor facility available in the event of inclement weather.

Meet with your staff and outline your rehearsal plan. Schedule blocks of time to cover various aspects in your plan i.e. warm-ups, tuning, music sectionals, full ensemble playing, stretching, marching fundamentals, and final performance run-throughs. If you're rehearsing your half-time show have extra adults available to assist with your podium and pit equipment as well as any props you may be using. Give your staff their assignments and responsibilities for the rehearsal. In the event of inclement weather have a "plan B" for an indoor rehearsal.

Prepare for your performance months before your departure so you can use the rehearsal time on the trip to simply review, refine and polish your performance.

Here are some essential items you should bring on the trip.

- Portable speaker system i.e. Long Ranger
- Instrument repair kit
- Tuner
- Reeds
- Valve oil
- Extra drumheads, drumsticks and mallets
- Drum keys
- Stick tape
- Extra flags, poles, rifles, pompoms, hoops and other props
- Duct Tape
- Electrical ties
- 100' Tape measure
- Yardline markers
- Orange cones
- Equipment to line a field

Returning Home

When you finally arrive back at the school everyone will be anxious to get off the bus and head for home to share their memories and rest. On the ride home have your students call their parents when you're one hour from the school to alert them of your anticipated arrival time. When you're within a few miles of the school have students begin to gather all their personal items and police the area around their seats for any garbage. Have the chaperones walk through the bus from back to front with a large trash bag to collect the garbage.

When you arrive keep everyone on the bus until the chaperones have checked the overhead compartments and completed a walkthrough of the bus and are satisfied with the condition the students have left things in. Excuse the students and check the bus once again. No doubt you'll probably still find a few items that students have left behind. Gather up the items and place them in a lost and found box in the band room.

In their hurry to leave someone will probably grab the wrong luggage and you'll have other students looking frantically for theirs. This situation usually resolves itself pretty quickly especially if a guy arrives home and opens the suitcase to find girl's clothing.

On the first day back to school following your trip give the students an opportunity to bring in their photos to share with each other and reminisce about their experience. Now that everyone's home again safe and sound you too can relax and reflect on the opportunity you've provided for your students. When they're adults and look back at their time in school you can rest assured that these are the moments they'll remember and cherish the most. Funny thing though now that I've retired from teaching all those trips I made with my students are the things I now remember and cherish the most!

Trip Follow-up

A week or two after you return from the trip survey your students, parents, chaperones and staff for their overall impression of the trip. Ask their opinion on the quality of service provided by the various vendors including transportation, housing, meals, sightseeing, entertainment, and the performance opportunity. What things did they like? What didn't they like? How could the experience have been better? Is this an event we should return to in the future?

Your Travel Company will send you a similar survey to complete for their follow-up report.

Some Final Thoughts

- Be prepared! Expect the unexpected!
- Always have a "Plan B"!
- Treat students with respect and they will return the favor!
- Students prefer structure even though they will never admit it!
- When traveling during the winter months advise your students to get a Flu shot.
- Discuss money management with your students.
- Suggest a dollar amount for parents to send on the trip with their student.
- Have an emergency cash fund available to cover miscellaneous expenses, unforeseen problems and to loan students if they lose their wallet or purse.
- Hire a photographer or recruit an interested parent to document your trip and put together a memory DVD for your students.

Resources

Website Links

Pasadena Tournament of Roses Official site—http://www.tournamentofroses.com/
Macy's Thanksgiving Day Parade Official site—http://social.macys.com/parade/#/home
Fort McDowell Fiesta Bowl Parade—http://www.fiestabowl.org/events/fiesta-bowl-parade.php
Marching.com—http://marching.com/
Transportation Safety Authority website—http://www.tsa.gov/
Seat Guru—http://www.seatguru.com/
American Bus Association—http://www.buses.org/
Music for All—http://www.musicforall.org/
National Travel Association—http://www.ntaonline.com/
Group Photos, Inc.—http://www.groupphotos.com/

Major Events List

Macy's Thanksgiving Day Parade—New York, New York
Philadelphia Thanksgiving Day Parade—Philadelphia, Pennsylvania
McDonald's Thanksgiving Day Parade—Chicago, Illinois
Americas Thanksgiving Parade—Detroit Michigan
Thanksgiving Parade of Bands at the Walt Disney World® Resort—Orlando, Florida
Waikiki Holiday Parade—Honolulu, Hawaii
West Chester Old Fashioned Christmas Parade—West Chester, Pennsylvania
America's Children's Holiday Parade—Oakland, California
Pearl Harbor Memorial Parade—Honolulu, Hawaii
Fiesta Bowl Parade and Fiesta Bowl Band Championship—Phoenix, Arizona
Pasadena Tournament of Roses Parade—Pasadena, California
Florida Citrus Parade—Orlando, Florida
Rome New Year's Parade—Rome, Italy
Honolulu Festival Parade of Bands—Honolulu, Hawaii
New York City St. Patrick's Day Parade—New York, NY
Chicago St. Patrick's Day Parade—Chicago, Illinois
Pittsburgh St. Patrick's Day Parade—Pittsburgh, Pennsylvania
National Cherry Blossom Festival Parade—Washington, D.C.
National Memorial Day Parade—Washington, D.C.
D-Day Anniversary—Normandy, France
Portland Rose Festival Grand Floral Parade—Portland, Oregon
National Independence Day Parade—Washington, D.C.
Philadelphia Independence Day Parade—Philadelphia, Pennsylvania
Calgary Stampede Parade and Show Bands Live—Calgary, Alberta, Canada

NYC Veterans Day Parade and Band of Pride Tribute—New York, New York
San Diego Veterans Day Parade and Band of Pride Tribute—San Diego, California
Magnificent Mile Lights Festival Parade—Chicago, Illinois
Kentucky Derby Festival Pegasus Parade—Louisville, Kentucky
Hollywood Christmas Parade—Hollywood, California
Santa Claus Parade—Toronto, Canada

Travel Associations

Music for All

One of the largest and most influential national music education organizations, actively involved in support of active music-making, Music for All uniquely combines national level programming and awareness campaigns, research and advocacy. Bands of America, Orchestra America and BOA Summer Symposium are three of Music for All's best-known programs.

Disney Parks Recognized Youth Travel Planner

The Recognized Youth Travel Planner designation and logo is a Mark of Excellence awarded by Walt Disney Parks & Resorts to its top youth travel partners. It comes with a travel company's selection to participate in the prestigious Walt Disney World Resort/Disneyland Resort Youth Travel Planner Symposium.

The American Bus Association

ABA (American Bus Association) is the trade association of the intercity bus industry. Active in representing members' interests before the U.S. Government, it also facilitates relationships between North American motor coach and tour companies. Promoting motor coach travel to consumers is a major ABA focus.

National Tour Association

NTA is made up of over 600 professional tour companies and allied travel suppliers. NTA members must carry a minimum of $1 million dollars of professional liability insurance coverage, and each must have had two years' experience in tour operations.

Sample Forms and Letters

Feel free to modify and duplicate any of the following letters or forms for your own use. If you would like the Microsoft Word files for any of the letters or forms listed below send a request to the following email address and I will forward them to you. Ayaracs@outlook.com

Housing Form
Hotel Room Inspection Form
Packing Checklist
Packing Checklist for Commercial or Charter Air Travel
Luggage & Carry-on Bag Check—Parent Verification Form / use if this is your first trip
Luggage & Carry-on Bag Check—Parent Verification Form
Luggage & Carry-on Bag Check—Parent Verification Form / Air Travel
Emergency Medical Release Form (pg. 1)
Student Health History—Emergency Medical Release Form (pg. 2)
Student Contract
Trip Announcement Letter (pg. 1)
Trip Announcement Letter (pg. 2)
Student Trip Account Loan Agreement
Band Chaperone & Medical Personnel Interest Form
Departure Day—Chaperone Trip Information
Final Parent Trip Meeting Agenda
Student Trip Guidelines
Permission For Alternate Transportation
Tips on preparing an application
Sample Parade Block—Television Area
56 Passenger Bus Seating Diagram
Sample Certificate of Insurance

(Event name)

HOUSING FORM

This form is to be completed by the Room Captain and must include 3 additional names. The room captain will be issued the key cards and is responsible for completing a room inspection form upon arrival. Please note if your room list does not contain 4 names you will be reassigned with other students that do not have a complete room.

ROOM CAPTAIN _____ Grade _____

Roommate #2 _____ Grade _____

Roommate #3 _____ Grade _____

Roommate #4 _____ Grade _____

. . . .

Cut here

(Event name)

HOUSING FORM

This form is to be completed by the Room Captain and must include 3 additional names. The room captain will be issued the key cards and is responsible for completing a room inspection form upon arrival. Please note if your room list does not contain 4 names you will be reassigned with other students that do not have a complete room.

ROOM CAPTAIN _____ Grade _____

Roommate #2 _____ Grade _____

Roommate #3 _____ Grade _____

Roommate #4 _____ Grade _____

(Event name)

Hotel Room Inspection Form

Students Name _____ Room # _____
(Room Captain)

Date of inspection _____ Time _____

Overall room cleanliness: *(circle one)*   Excellent   Good   Fair   Poor

Are there sufficient towels, washcloths & toiletries for quad occupancy?   Yes   No

List any noticeable damage to: doors, walls, carpet, window treatments, furniture, lights, bathroom fixtures, beds, bed linens, pillows, alarm clock, hairdryer, coffee maker, mini fridge, and television.

_____

_____

_____

_____

By initialing this form we the assigned students in this room verify the accuracy of the information provided by our room captain.

Roommate 1 _____

Roommate 2 _____

Roommate 3 _____

This form will be kept on file until after the group successfully checks out of the hotel

(Event name)

PACKING CHECKLIST

Luggage restrictions: each student is permitted one small carry-on bag and one small piece of luggage. Make sure both your carry-on bag and luggage are labeled. You are responsible for handling your own luggage during the trip.

Band Uniform Checklist: Band bag & Garment Bag (labeled)

- ☐ Garment Bag with your uniform coat & pants on the uniform hanger
- ☐ Band Bag with your shako or helmet in the hat box, Drillmaster shoes, black socks, black gloves, band raincoat
- ☐ Pack anything else you may need for under your uniform i.e. under armor in your luggage.

Auxiliary Unit Checklist: Band bag & Garment Bag (labeled)

- ☐ Band bag with your performance shoes in a plastic bag, makeup, hairspray/gel and extra bobby pins, hair ties, performance bra, body tights, nude leotard and raincoat
- ☐ Uniform in a garment bag on the uniform hanger

Recommended Items:

- ☐ Watch or cell phone / time management is important on band trips
- ☐ Toothbrush, Toothpaste, Dental Floss, Mouthwash
- ☐ Deodorant
- ☐ Comb, Hairbrush, Hairspray, Gel, Sponge Rollers, Shampoo, Conditioner, Curling Iron, all rooms have built in hair dryers
- ☐ Cologne, Perfume, Hand Cream (*makeup & personal items for girls*)
- ☐ Q-Tips, Kleenex
- ☐ Contac lens cleaner, saline solution, eye drops or eyeglass cleaner for those that need it
- ☐ Shaving Items: electric razor, razor blades must be safety razors, shaving cream or gel
- ☐ Medicine, vitamins / please inform the band nurses of any prescription drugs your student must bring
- ☐ Underwear—Sleepwear / Slippers
- ☐ Casual clothes blue jeans are recommended—PLEASE NOTE: nothing on our itinerary requires formal dress
- ☐ Comfortable shoes & socks

Optional Items:

- ☐ Cell phone
- ☐ Camera & Film / throw away cameras work well
- ☐ Reading material, magazines, for on the bus
- ☐ IPod, portable DVD player, bring these items at your own risk and responsibility / must use with headphones on the bus
- ☐ Small pillow & blanket for use on the bus
- ☐ Snack food, all drinks must be in sealed containers and packed in your carry-on bag
- ☐ Miscellaneous cash for souvenirs and snacks—dollar amount at your parent's discretion

(Event name)
Packing Checklist for Commercial or Charter Air Travel

Luggage restrictions: each student is permitted one carry-on bag and one large suitcase (your checked bag must weigh less than 50 lbs.). A typical carry-on bag measures approximately 10" X 16" X 24" or may not exceed a total dimension of 45" when adding the length, width and height. Your suitcase is checked baggage that will go under the plane and will not be accessible during your flight. Please refrain from locking your checked baggage or use a TSA "accepted and recognized" lock. Make sure both your carry-on and checked baggage is labeled.

Tips for packing your checked baggage as recommended by the Transportation Security Administration:
- Don't put film in your checked baggage, as the screening equipment will damage it
- Pack shoes, boots, sneakers, and other footwear on top of the other contents in your luggage
- Avoid packing food and drink items in your checked baggage
- Avoid over packing so that your articles don't spill out if your bag is opened for inspection
- Do not pack or bring prohibited items to the airport—box cutters, knives, and scissors

Tips for packing your carry-on bag as recommended by the Transportation Security Administration:
- Put all undeveloped film and cameras with film in your carry-on baggage
- Do not pack or bring prohibited items to the airport—box cutters, knives, and scissors
- Think carefully about the personal items you place in the carry-on baggage. The screeners may have to open your bag and examine its contents

3-1-1 for carry-ons = 3 ounce bottles or less; 1 quart sized, clear plastic, zip-top bag: 1 bag per passenger placed in screening bin. One-quart bag per person limits the total liquid volume each traveler can bring. 3 oz. container size is a security measure. If in doubt put your liquids in your checked luggage. Nail files and nail clippers are also allowed in checked or carryon baggage. The airline recommends that customers carry their medications in carryon baggage and that medications requiring refrigeration are cooled with nontoxic gel packs. Medications should be transported in original pharmacy packaging that includes the customer's name. If this is not possible, please carry a copy of the prescription for the medication. We permit all diabetes-related supplies and other injectable medications such as insulin, hypodermic needles, pens, lancets, pumps, jet injectors, and syringes to be carried onboard. Insulin must have the pharmaceutical or manufacturer's name printed on the label.

Recommended Items:
- ☐ Watch or cell phone—time management is important on band trips
- ☐ Toothbrush, Toothpaste, Dental Floss, Mouthwash etc.
- ☐ Deodorant
- ☐ Comb, Hairbrush, Hairspray, Gel, Sponge Rollers, Shampoo, Conditioner, Curling Iron, as needed / all rooms have built in hair dryers
- ☐ Cologne, Aftershave, Perfume, Hand Cream (*personal items for girls*), etc.
- ☐ Q-Tips, Kleenex
- ☐ Shaving Items: razor blades must be safety razors, shaving cream or gel
- ☐ Medicine, vitamins / please inform our band nurses of any prescription drugs your student must bring
- ☐ Underwear (enough for ___ days)—Sleepwear / Slippers
- ☐ Casual clothes for (___) days blue jeans are recommended—nothing on our itinerary requires formal dress
- ☐ Comfortable shoes & socks (*enough for ___ days*)
- ☐ Sweatshirts or light sweaters for evening wear

Optional Items:
- ☐ Cell phone
- ☐ Shorts
- ☐ Swimsuit
- ☐ Camera & Film / throw away cameras work well—there will be lots of great photo opportunities!
- ☐ Reading material for in the airport and on the plane
- ☐ Money for snacks, shopping and or souvenirs $(___) / all meals are provided on this trip

(Event name)—use this form if this is your first trip

Luggage & Carry-on Bag Check—Parent Verification Form

I am looking forward to our first overnight band trip on *(date)*. Student travel opportunities are a privilege and serve to enhance the class curriculum. The school board has validated their trust in our students and has approved our trip.

I share their belief. Band students are among the best students in our school but even they can fall prey to temptation and make poor choices. There is no possible way we can efficiently check each and every piece of luggage brought on the trip so I am asking for your help in this matter.

All school rules apply on our trip so please check your student luggage and verify it does not contain any TOBACCO PRODUCTS, ALCOHOL, SUSPECTED CONTROLLED SUBSTANCE, and OR WEAPONS. I'm sure you will agree that if any student were found with these items it would be a source of great embarrassment for their parents as well as a great disappointment to the administration, their fellow band members and the band staff.

Once you have checked both pieces of luggage please sign and date this form. Your student should turn this form in to their chaperones when they arrive on *(departure date)*. Unfortunately we will have to inspect the bags of those students that don't return a form. This could be very time consuming, embarrassing to the student and greatly impact our scheduled departure time. In order to prevent any delay in our scheduled departure and eliminate the potential for problems on the trip your help and cooperation in this matter is appreciated. Thank you in advance for your support!

Sincerely,
(signature)
Band Director

I have checked my student's luggage and carry-on bag and verify that it does not contain: TOBACCO PRODUCTS, ALCOHOL, SUSPECTED CONTROLLED SUBSTANCE, and OR WEAPONS. I UNDERSTAND THAT IF MY STUDENT WERE TO VIOLATE THIS RULE THEY WILL IMMEDIATELY BE EXCLUDED FROM PARTICIPATING IN ANY FURTHER MARCHING BAND ACTIVITIES. IF AN INCIDENT OCCURS THE APPROPRIATE SCHOOL OFFICIALS (Principal, Superintendent), WILL BE IMMEDIATELY NOTIFIED AND CURRENT (_____*school district*) POLICIES GOVERNING THE OFFENSE WILL BE ENFORCED. PENALTIES FOR SUCH OFFENSES MAY INCLUDE EXPULSION, SUSPENSION, FINES AND PERMANENT REMOVAL FROM THE BAND PROGRAM.

Student's Name(s) _____ Grade(s) _____

Parent's Signature _____ Date _____

Families with more than one member can list them all on one form

(Event name)

Luggage & Carry-on Bag Check—Parent Verification Form

Student travel opportunities are a privilege and serve to enhance the class curriculum. The (_____*band*) has enjoyed (___) years of successful student travel. Our students have always represented their parents, our school and the (_____) community with "PRIDE".

On occasion a few students have made poor choices that necessitated their permanent removal from the band. In addition some faced expulsion or suspension from school and fines. Needless to say their poor judgment was a source of great embarrassment to them and their parents as well as a great disappointment to the administration, their fellow band members and the band staff. There is no possible way we can efficiently check each and every piece of luggage brought on a trip so I am asking for your help in this matter.

Once you have checked both pieces of luggage please sign and date this form. Your student should turn this form in to their chaperones when they arrive on *(departure date)*. Unfortunately we will have to inspect the bags of those students that do not turn in a form. This could be very time consuming, embarrassing to the student and greatly impact our scheduled departure time. In order to prevent any delay in our scheduled departure and eliminate the potential for your student to have problems going through airport security your help and cooperation in this matter is appreciated. Thank you in advance for your support!

Sincerely,
(signature)
Band Director

I have checked my student's luggage and carry-on bag and verify that it does not contain: TOBACCO PRODUCTS, ALCOHOL, SUSPECTED CONTROLLED SUBSTANCE, and OR WEAPONS. I UNDERSTAND THAT IF MY STUDENT WERE TO VIOLATE THIS RULE THEY WILL IMMEDIATELY BE EXCLUDED FROM PARTICIPATING IN ANY FURTHER MARCHING BAND ACTIVITIES. IF AN INCIDENT OCCURS THE APPROPRIATE SCHOOL OFFICIALS (Principal, Superintendent), WILL BE IMMEDIATELY NOTIFIED AND CURRENT (_____*school district*) POLICIES GOVERNING THE OFFENSE WILL BE ENFORCED. PENALTIES FOR SUCH OFFENSES MAY INCLUDE EXPULSION, SUSPENSION, FINES AND PERMANENT REMOVAL FROM THE BAND PROGRAM.

Student's Name(s) _____ Grade(s) _____

Parent's Signature _____ Date _____

Families with more than one member can list them all on one form

Luggage & Carry-on Bag Check—Parent Verification Form / Air Travel

Student travel opportunities are a privilege and serve to enrich and enhance the class curriculum. The (_____*band*) has enjoyed (___) years of successful student travel. Our students have always represented their parents, school and the (_____) community with "PRIDE".

On occasion a few students have made poor choices that necessitated their permanent removal from the band. In addition some faced expulsion or suspension from school and fines. Needless to say their poor judgment was a source of great embarrassment to them and their parents as well as a great disappointment to the administration, their fellow band members and the band staff. There is no possible way we can efficiently check each and every piece of luggage brought on a trip so I am asking for your help in this matter. Additional care must be taken because of airport security and luggage restrictions. Please take time to help your student pack their luggage and carry-on bag. Visit the TSA Website at www.tsa.gov and review the instructions for properly packing your carryon bag (3-1-1).

Once you have checked both pieces of luggage please sign and date this form. Your student should turn this form in to their chaperones when they arrive on (*departure date*). Unfortunately we will have to inspect the bags of those students that do not turn in a form. This could be very time consuming, embarrassing to the student and greatly impact our scheduled departure time. In order to prevent any delay in our scheduled departure and eliminate the potential for your student to have problems going through airport security your help and cooperation in this matter is appreciated. Thank you in advance for your support!

Sincerely,
(signature)
Band Director

_____

I have checked my student's luggage and carry-on bag and verify that it meets the TSA packing guidelines and does not contain: TOBACCO PRODUCTS, ALCOHOL, SUSPECTED CONTROLLED SUBSTANCE, and OR WEAPONS. I UNDERSTAND THAT IF MY STUDENT WERE TO VIOLATE THIS RULE THEY WILL IMMEDIATELY BE EXCLUDED FROM PARTICIPATING IN ANY FURTHER MARCHING BAND ACTIVITIES. IF AN INCIDENT OCCURS THE APPROPRIATE SCHOOL OFFICIALS (Principal, Superintendent), WILL BE IMMEDIATELY NOTIFIED AND CURRENT (_____*school district*) POLICIES GOVERNING THE OFFENSE WILL BE ENFORCED. PENALTIES FOR SUCH OFFENSES MAY INCLUDE EXPULSION, SUSPENSION, FINES AND PERMANENT REMOVAL FROM THE BAND PROGRAM.

Student's Name(s) _____ Grade(s) _____

Parent's Signature _____ Date _____

Families with more than one member can list them all on one form

(Band name)   *Attach student photo here*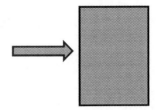

EMERGENCY MEDICAL RELEASE FORM *(pg. 1)*

Student's Name _____ Date of Birth _____ Male / Female

Grade _____ Football Season Bus #_____ (to be completed by Nurses) Trip Bus #_____

As the parent(s)/guardian(s) of the above-named student, I/we on behalf of myself/ourselves, my/our heirs, executors, administrators, and assigns, and on behalf of the above-named student do hereby release and discharge the (school district name), its employees, agents and/or servants from any and all rights, claims, and/or actions which I/we and or the above-named student may hereafter have against the (_____*school district*), employees, agents and/or servants arising out of traveling and performing with the (_____*band*).

I understand that in case of a medical emergency, every reasonable attempt will be made to contact the parent(s)/guardian(s) of the above-named student. If, however, I/we cannot be contacted and a medical emergency arises, I/we by affixing my/our signature(s) to this form give permission for my/our child to receive all necessary emergency medical care.

_____ Date _____
Signature(s) of Parent(s)/Guardian(s)

_____ Phone _____
Address

_____ Phone _____
Place of employment, if applicable

_____ Phone _____
Additional person to contact if parent/guardian is not at home

IN CASE OF EMERGENCY ROOM CARE, PLEASE PROVIDE THE FOLLOWING:

a) Insurance policy number _____

b) Insurance company _____

c) Family physician _____ Phone _____

Is your child currently on any medication?   Yes _____ No _____ Specify _____

Has your child had a tetanus injection?   Yes _____ No _____ Date of Last Injection _____

Known allergies? _____

Student Health History—Emergency Medical Form *(pg. 2)*

TO BE COMPLETED BY A PARENT—PLEASE ANSWER ALL QUESTIONS

My child has had (or currently has), the following medical condition(s):

CIRCLE ONE

A.	RHEUMATIC FEVER OR SCARLET FEVER	YES	NO
B.	SEIZURE OR CONVULSIVE DISORDER	YES	NO
C.	ANEMIA (INCLUDING SICKLE CELL ANEMIA)	YES	NO
D.	MONONUCLEOSIS OR HEPATITIS	YES	NO
E.	ASTHMA	YES	NO
F.	DIABETES	YES	NO
G.	HIGH BLOOD PRESSURE	YES	NO
H.	KIDNEY DISEASE	YES	NO
I.	RETINAL DETACHMENT OR EYE DISORDER	YES	NO
J.	ABSENCE OF PAIRED ORGAN (KIDNEY, ETC.)	YES	NO
K.	CONCUSSION (IF YES, HOW MANY TIMES) #_____	YES	NO
L.	THYROID DISEASE	YES	NO
M.	GASTROINTESTINAL DISEASE	YES	NO

My child:

HAD AN ILLNESS LASTING MORE THAN ONE WEEK?	YES	NO
HAS BEEN IN THE HOSPITAL (EXCEPT TONSILLECTOMY)?	YES	NO
HAS HAD SURGERY?	YES	NO
HAS HAD TETANUS IMMUNIZATION? Date	YES	NO
WEARS GLASSES OR CONTACT LENS?	YES	NO
HAS HAD LOWER BACK PAIN?	YES	NO
HAD AN INJURY OF A MUSCLE, BONE, JOINT, LIGAMENT OR TENDON?	YES	NO
HAS A HISTORY OF FAINTING RELATING TO EXERCISE?	YES	NO
HAS ALLERGIES?	YES	NO

ALLERGY MEDICATION _____

IS CURRENTLY ON MEDICATION?	YES	NO

NAME OF MEDICATION_____

IS CURRENTLY UNDER A PHYSICIAN'S CARE?	YES	NO

PHYSICIAN_____

PLEASE INDICATE ANY OTHER IMPORTANT MEDICAL INFORMATION WE SHOULD KNOW ABOUT BELOW

_____

_____

_____

(Band name)
Student Contract *(year)*

Return this form with your completed Emergency Medical Release Form

Student's Name _____ Grade _____
(PLEASE PRINT)

Instrument/Position _____

I WILL NOT POSSESS OR USE ANY TOBACCO PRODUCTS, ALCOHOL, SUSPECTED CONTROLLED SUBSTANCE, OR WEAPONS DURING ANY MARCHING BAND FUNCTION.

I UNDERSTAND THAT IF I VIOLATE THIS RULE I WILL IMMEDIATELY BE EXCLUDED FROM PARTICIPATING IN ANY FURTHER MARCHING BAND ACTIVITIES. WHEN A VIOLATION IS REPORTED THE (_____*school district*) POLICIES GOVERNING THE OFFENSE WILL BE ENFORCED AND THE APPROPRIATE SCHOOL OFFICIALS (Principal, Superintendent), WILL BE IMMEDIATELY NOTIFIED.

I WILL TREAT MY FELLOW BAND MEMBERS, CHAPERONES, MEDICAL STAFF, AND DIRECTORS WITH RESPECT. I UNDERSTAND THE SCHOOL DISTRICT POLICIES REGARDING HAZING, PROFANITY, DISRESPECT AND SEXUAL HARASSMENT.

I UNDERSTAND THAT IF I VIOLATE ANY OF THE BAND POLICIES I MAY BE SUSPENDED FROM PARTICIPATING IN ACTIVITIES AND PERFORMING WITH THE BAND AND APPROPRIATE DISCIPLINARY ACTION IN ACCORDANCE WITH (_____*school district*) POLICIES WILL BE TAKEN.

I have carefully read all of the information above and in the marching band student handbook and my commitment, responsibilities, and the policies that pertain to my membership in the marching band.

I agree to abide by all of the policies stated above and in the handbook.

I will put forth my best effort in all that I do to continue the success and fine tradition of the (_____*band*) and to be present for all band activities.

Student's Name _____ Grade _____

Parent/Guardian Signature _____ Date _____

STUDENTS THAT FAIL TO TURN IN A COMPLETED CONTRACT
WILL BE DROPPED FROM THE BAND ROSTER

Trip Announcement Letter

Dear parents,

On (date) the school board reviewed and approved plans for a band trip to (*destination*) for the (*event*) on (*date*). All arrangements listed below are courtesy of (_____*travel Company*) our travel provider. The cost per student for this trip is itemized below for your review.

Transportation: (*charter bus, commercial air or charter air information if applicable and cost*) per person.

Land Package: Pricing based on our current membership: $(____) per student quad occupancy.

Included features

- (____) nights' accommodations at the (_____*hotel*)
- Visit the hotel website at (www. _____)
- All hotel taxes
- All meals
- All motor coach transportation as per itinerary
- List the included itinerary, sightseeing and admissions below:
  - ✓ _____
  - ✓ _____
  - ✓ _____
  - ✓ _____
  - ✓ _____
- $(____) liability insurance per person per occurrence

$(____) Transportation
$(____) Land Package
$(____) (*include any additional costs here*)
$(____) Total cost per student

Payment Schedule:

(date) $(____) initial non-refundable deposit
(date) $(____) Payment #2
(date) $(____) Payment #3
(date) $(____) Payment #4
(date) $(____) Final Balance due
        $(____) Total

The $(____) non-refundable initial deposit is extremely important because it will establish our final numbers for the trip and lock in all costs. Please contact me if you have any questions.

In order to help students earn funds towards their trip the following fundraising projects are scheduled. Our new fundraising chairperson is (_____). If you are available to help with product distributions please contact (_____) at (000) 000-0000 or via email @ (*email address*).

(letterhead)

Fundraising Schedule:

Month—Date—Insert project information
Month—Date—Insert project information
Month—Date—Insert project information
Month—Date—Insert project information
Month—Date—Insert project information
Month—Date—Insert project information
Month—Date—Insert project information
Month—Date—Insert project information

In addition to the projects listed above the band will sponsor (*additional projects*) and is looking into local restaurant fundraisers where a percentage of the meals purchased on a particular evening go to the band. I would encourage your student to take advantage of as many of these opportunities as possible and get a head start on building their trip account now.

We currently have (____) families with two or more students in the band. Over the next few months the boosters and I will explore ways to try to provide some form of assistance.

(_____*travel Company*) is putting together a Family & Friends package for parents who might like to travel to (destination) for this "once in a lifetime" event. The package would include transportation, hotel, meals, sightseeing and the opportunity to enjoy the bands performance. As soon as this information is finalized we will make it available to you. Book early space will be limited.

Please do not hesitate to contact me if you have any questions.

Sincerely,

(signature)
Band Director

Visit the band website @ (www. _____) for all the latest information and fundraiser reminders

STUDENT TRIP ACCOUNT LOAN AGREEMENT
(letterhead)
(Band Director's Name)
(School Address)
(Band Office Phone #)
(Email Address)

(date)

(parent's name)
(address)

Dear (_____),

This letter is in response to our recent phone conversation regarding *(student's name)* *(event name)* student trip account. Due to your current financial circumstance the band boosters are willing to offer a loan to pay the balance on *(student's name)* trip account so *(student's name)* may participate in the band trip. As per our phone conversation you have agreed to make monthly payments over the next (_____) months to pay the loan back in full by *(date)*. If the entire loan is not repaid by *(date)* the remaining balance will be turned into the school office as a student obligation.

If you find the terms of this agreement workable please date, sign and return one copy ASAP. Keep the other copy for your files. Once I receive your signed agreement I will have our band treasurer pay the balance owed on *(student's name)* account to the travel company.

I realize this matter is a sensitive issue and it will be kept confidential. I am glad *(student's name)* will be able to participate in the trip.

Sincerely,

(signature)
Band Director

Band Student Account Loan Agreement
(band name)

With my signature below I agree to the terms and conditions of this agreement and will pay back the loan in the amount of $(_____) over the next (_____) months with payment in full no later than *(date)*.

There will be a total of (___) payments due on the *(date)* of each month in the amount of (___) dollars with final payment in full no later than *(date)*.

Payment 1—*(date)* Payment 2—*(date)* Payment 3—*(date)* Payment 4—*(date)* Final payment *(date)*

Parent's Signature _____ Date _____

Band Director's Signature _____ Date _____

Sign, date and return one copy—keep the other copy for your files.

(letterhead)

Band Chaperone & Medical Personnel Interest Form

Two of the most important types of volunteers for the band program are chaperones and medical personnel. Without these people our program couldn't function. Each year we lose senior chaperone couples and nurses, EMT's or paramedics through student graduation. This year we'll need to replace (__) medical personnel and (__) chaperone couples to maintain the proper adult to student supervision ratio. For your protection as well as the students we require our chaperones and medical personnel to obtain criminal background and child abuse clearances from the state. A copy of these forms must be on file in the band office before the first trip each season.

Clearance Information and applications are available on the (_____) Website: (_____)

Act (____) Request for Criminal Record Check—$(__) Fee
Act (____) Child Abuse History Clearances—$(__) Fee

Chaperones are assigned to the same bus and group of students for the entire season. We generally place two couples on each bus as a team with the exception of the busses with band staff on them. Commitments this year include (_____). Consult the band schedule available on our website for the exact dates and times for these events. Medical personnel will work as a team to assist the band staff and handle medical issues at all band performances and band camp.

If you're interested in helping in either capacity please fill out the form below and return it ASAP. I will contact you by phone or e-mail to confirm receipt of your form and discuss your involvement in our program. Chaperone and medical personnel positions are one year obligations with an option to return the next year if interested and approved by the head chaperones and band director. There will be a special meeting before the season begins to give everyone on our team a chance to meet each other and review our rules and supervision policies and procedures.

Sincerely,

(signature)
Band Director

Band Chaperone & Medical Personnel Interest Form

Name(s) _____ Phone _____

E-mail: _____

Student's Name(s) _____ Grade(s) _____

☐ We are interested in volunteering as chaperones for the (____) band season.
☐ I am a certified (Nurse EMT Paramedic) and interested in volunteering for the (____) band season.
Circle one

Mail this form to: (_____)

Chaperones should plan to arrive at the high school auditorium by (_____) on (*day, date*) to supervise students when they arrive at (_____). The building will be open at (_____) if you choose to come early. Each bus will be assigned a specific area in the auditorium where chaperones will meet their students.

After unloading your luggage park your car in the (_____*parking lot*). Make sure your car is locked, lights are off and you have your keys. Place your luggage in the auditorium lobby. You'll be boarding the bus ahead of the students. As students arrive take roll and report any absentees. Make sure students have their band windbreaker with them and it is not packed in their suitcase. They'll need to wear it whenever they're off of the bus, (*in the airport*) and out of the hotel complex.

After a brief meeting at (_____) I will send all chaperones out to the busses to get situated. Once you're ready I will begin to excuse the student's one bus at a time for loading and boarding. All male chaperones should assist with loading the luggage in the bins under the bus. Student volunteers will be available to help you. Students must fill in every seat from the back of the bus forward. Each of you will have two seats to yourself in the front of the bus. Students do not have assigned seats only an assigned bus. They must always ride the same bus unless moved by (*band director*) due to a medical or disciplinary issue.

Take roll each time students re-board the bus during the trip. A headcount is sufficient and faster. If you find you're missing students then call the roll. Choose one chaperone on each bus to take roll throughout the entire trip. I will provide you with roll sheets, a laminated bus number, and a pen and clipboard on (departure date). Whenever students exit the buses remind them to always stay in groups of four or more.

When we arrive at the hotel a representative will give you instructions on their procedure for distributing the room key cards to your students. Before the students get off of the bus remind them that they are responsible for handling their own luggage throughout the trip.

Once you've checked in I will meet with you to review our plans for the remainder of the day and explain the procedure for checking rooms at curfew each night. Throughout the trip I will meet with you to review the necessary information for the day.

While in the hotel chaperones will be responsible for a specific group of student rooms on their floor. In most cases the students in these rooms will be different than the ones you supervise on the bus. You will get a room list to help you. Each evening following our room checks security guards will take over supervision for the night.

Our nurse's rooms will be blocked together and located beside the sick rooms on the same floor as the girls. We will have two sick rooms available.

In order to preserve the battery on our two-way radios turn them off while in transit and turn them back on again when you get off of the bus. Each evening we'll collect the radios for charging. Two-way radios will be assigned to the staff and several chaperones for the duration of the trip. Everyone will get a cell phone list. Program the numbers in your phone ahead of time to expedite your ability make an emergency call if needed.

When our truck arrives at the hotel we will need your help in unloading and organizing the uniforms and equipment in the designated storage area.

Attitude is everything! No matter how well planned a trip is there is always the unexpected. We will do our best to work through any problems that may arise. Your help maintaining a positive attitude around the students in these situations is appreciated. I've told the students many times that whenever we travel they should learn to expect the unexpected, be flexible, and just go with the flow and enjoy the trip. If you have any questions or concerns during the trip please bring them to my attention.

THANK YOU FOR YOUR HELP AND SUPPORT AND ALL THAT YOU DO FOR THE STUDENTS!

FINAL PARENT TRIP MEETING AGENDA

(Meeting Date & Location)

Medical Issues:
- ✓ If you have had any changes in student medical information or insurance coverage—please see our nurses tonight with your changes.
- ✓ If your student will be traveling with prescription drugs—we will need documentation indicating the prescription your student is taking and the reason they need the medication. All prescription drugs must be in the original containers and students should only bring enough of the medication needed to cover the duration of our trip. Exceptions may apply to some liquid medications i.e. cough medications in measured bottles. If anything would change before our departure please send this information with your student on *(departure date)*.
- ✓ Students must never share non-prescription medications.
- ✓ Medical forms will be handled by the chaperones on each bus throughout the trip itinerary.
- ✓ Each student will be provided a copy of their medical form to wear under their uniform on parade day.
- ✓ Parade first aid and medical policies? Water during the parade route? Restroom availability before and after the parade?
- ✓ What happens if your student becomes sick during the trip? Sick rooms. Parade participation?
- ✓ Food allergies and concerns: allergies, vegetarians, peanut oil etc.

Additional Items:
- ✓ (_____*school district*) liability forms must be on file with the school district before we depart you may turn them in tonight.
- ✓ (include if flying) Student Photo I.D.'s chaperones will distribute and collect these during the trip.
- ✓ Student reporting time is (_____) on *(day, date)*. Anyone leaving a car on campus must park in the (_____*parking lot*). Students should wear comfortable casual clothes for travel. Blue jeans, a sweatshirt or sweater, comfortable shoes and socks and the band windbreaker. Students must wear the band windbreaker to aid in group supervision when off the charter coaches. Students are permitted one carryon bag and one regular suitcase *(they are responsible for handling both of these items throughout the entire trip)*.
- ✓ (*include if flying*) Visit the TSA Website at: www.tsa.gov for detailed information on 3-1-1 proper packing guidelines for carryon luggage. This site is linked from the band website.
- ✓ Flight Information, luggage restrictions and TSA regulations—label all items
- ✓ Trip Itinerary—to view and print the entire trip itinerary go to the information on the band website.
- ✓ Review of the trip packing guide & checklist—casual clothing, spending money, cell phones, iPods, cameras
- ✓ We will be loading our uniforms and equipment on the truck on (insert date & time) any help would be appreciated.
- ✓ Prior to the parade (_____*photo company*) will take a staged group photo which will be available for purchase. They will provide information to the students.

Review of student behavior & trip guidelines
- ✓ All (_____ *school district*) Rules & Policies governing student behavior will apply.
- ✓ Students are expected to follow the instructions from the band staff, chaperones, bus drivers, travel company representatives, hotel staff and event officials.
- ✓ Only the 4 roommates assigned to a room are permitted in that room and on that floor.
- ✓ Students may not leave the hotel at any time with visiting relatives.
- ✓ Students must adhere to all hotel policies & rules—video surveillance cameras.
- ✓ Students must follow the scheduled evening curfew time.
- ✓ Security guards will be on duty overnight.
- ✓ Damage to any hotel room or property will be assessed to the parent.
- ✓ We recommend students stay in groups of 4 or more when we are out and about.

Closing remarks—if you have any questions please see me after the meeting or you may call the band office

STUDENT TRIP GUIDELINES

Student reporting time is (_____) on (*day, date*). Anyone leaving a car on campus must park in the (_____ *parking lot*) make sure your car is locked. Upon arrival find the designated location for your bus number in the auditorium and report to that area with your luggage. Check in with your chaperones. Students should wear comfortable casual clothes for travel such as blue jeans, a sweatshirt or sweater, comfortable shoes and socks and the band windbreaker. (*include if flying*) Avoid belts and clothing with lots of metal on them. Avoid wearing large heavy boots or bulky shoes. Snack food (gum, candy) may be packed in your carryon baggage but will be inspected when you go through security (bottled drinks will not be allowed through the security checkpoint). Refer to the TSA website packing guidelines www.tsa.gov link on the band website.

- ✓ Each student is responsible for carrying and loading their own luggage (carry-on bag and suitcase) throughout the duration of the trip.
- ✓ All students must wear the windbreaker to aid in group supervision.
- ✓ All (_____*school district*) Rules & Policies governing student behavior will apply.
- ✓ Students are expected to follow the instructions from the band staff, chaperones, bus drivers, event staff, travel representatives, hotel staff & (*include if flying*) airline personnel, airport security; disrespect will not be tolerated.
- ✓ PDA—overt public display of affection is inappropriate and school policy will apply.
- ✓ Only the 4 roommates assigned to a room are permitted in that room and on that floor—under no circumstance should guys be in girl's rooms or floors or vice versa. There are numerous public areas at the hotel where you and your friends can get together and visit.
- ✓ Students may not leave the hotel at any time with visiting relatives.
- ✓ The hotel has video cameras throughout for your protection and we will have security guards on duty overnight.
- ✓ Students must follow all scheduled evening curfew times.
- ✓ Each evening a different nurse will be on call if you need medical attention.
- ✓ Damage to any hotel room or hotel property will be assessed to the parent.
- ✓ Students must always stay in groups of 4 or more when we are out and about.
- ✓ If a student becomes a discipline problem they will be sent home at their parent's expense.
- ✓ The (_____*hotel*) is a great facility—treat it with respect—there will be other guests in the hotel with us and I expect you to respect their privacy and watch noise levels—they paid a lot more than you did to stay at this hotel.
- ✓ You must be quiet, respectful and listen carefully to anyone that is giving you information or instructions on this trip
- ✓ (*include if flying*) You will get your photo ID on the bus. Chaperones will collect your photo ID after you clear security before boarding the plane.
- ✓ On parade day you must wear your medical lanyard under your uniform.
- ✓ Be on time or early when given bus departure or meeting times throughout the itinerary.
- ✓ Fill out the room check form upon arrival and report any hotel concerns immediately.

(letterhead)

PERMISSION FOR ALTERNATE TRANSPORTATION
Submit this form (___) days prior to the event.

Transportation to and from every band event is provided and students are expected to travel with the band. On occasion a circumstance may arise that requires alternate transportation. This form should be used to request permission to provide alternate transportation to (and or) from a band event. The person providing transportation must be the parent or an adult approved by the parent. Students will not be approved to travel with other students, boyfriends or girlfriends. Indicate your reason for requesting alternate transportation below. Be specific. You will be notified whether your request is approved or denied. If approved the individual providing transportation must assume all liability.

Date _____

Student's Name _____ Grade _____

Instrument or Position _____

I am requesting permission for alternate transportation for my son/daughter for the event listed below.

_____ on _____
EVENT   DATE

I would like my son/daughter to ride TO and/or FROM this event with _____
                                                      ADULT PROVIDING TRANSPORTATION

Reason for this request:_____
                                    Be specific

_____

_____

Parent's Signature _____ Phone # _____

E-mail: _____

Tips On Preparing An Application

An application tells the band's and director's story. Answer each item carefully be neat, accurate and concise. Most selection committees are usually comprised of parade experts, not necessarily band experts. They may not understand association abbreviations or the value of certain awards listed on your resume. Explain what each means.

SUBMITTING PHOTOGRAPHS

The photographs of your band in uniform present a clear image of how the band would appear and provide valuable showmanship information. Many bands take an annual group photo in uniform. This will fulfill the requirement for an 8x10 photograph of the entire band. In addition to a full band photograph include photographs that show your whole uniform, from the plume to the shoes. Show both the front and back of the uniform especially if there is a contrasting color and other feature noticeable once the band has passed. Include photos of the band, drum major, auxiliary units, and any variations in uniform. Don't rely on grainy photographs taken through a zoom lens at last year's homecoming field show. Make it easy. Ask a few students to dress in uniform and take posed photographs. Photos are generally not returned so keep copies for your files.

PREPARING YOUR DVD

A DVD gives the clearest idea of how your band would look and sound. Keep it simple. Focus on the band's sound as it passes how the uniforms look in motion, and precision marching. It's a good idea to avoid submitting clips of your band from a televised holiday or bowl parade where the broadcast announcers usually talk over the music. Make it all LIVE! Record the audio and visual simultaneously. Some of the most effective submissions show bands marching along a practice street or back and forth across the football field. If possible, demonstrate your band turning a corner. Position the camera slightly above the band if you can whether from the stands at the football stadium or from an overpass above the street. This helps assess marching precision and provides a better visual of the entire band. Balance distance with sound. As you strive for good visuals, keep audio in mind. Musicianship and overall sound are very important in the selection process. Don't be discouraged TV network productions have difficulty balancing band sound. Work with it a little and give it your best. Most events do not return materials so keep a copy for your files.

SUBMITTING LETTERS OF RECOMMENDATION

Use letters of recommendation to confirm and emphasize your band's strengths in musicianship, showmanship, dedication, consistency, and fundraising ability. Ask respected individuals. Consider people whose opinions carry weight, such as university band directors, festival or competition sponsors, politicians and education officials. Begin this process early. Because you're relying on important people, chances are they have busy schedules. Allow sufficient time to make the connections, gain the support, and receive the letters.

Begin preparing well in advance of the submission deadline. You will invest a significant amount of time assembling the components of your application. You'll need both straightforward items (such as numbers of participants, the bands accomplishments, and the directors experience), as well as items more difficult to orchestrate (such as letters of recommendation, assurance of adequate financial support, and a video of the entire band marching and playing in uniform). So begin early, talking to school officials and band booster groups, taking photographs and filming the video while the band is in prime marching form, and reestablishing the connections you'll need for the letters of recommendation. Consider designating an assistant director or booster club officer to help keep the process on track and on time. Give yourself time to represent your band at its best and to assemble an attention getting application.

CREATE A PORTFOLIO

Once you have gathered all of the necessary application materials it is a good idea to create a portfolio and present your information in as professional a manner as possible. A three ring binder with clear plastic sheet protectors works well. First impressions are important. Add an attractive eye catching cover and table of contents to make it easier for a committee to review your materials.

Sample Parade Block—Television Area

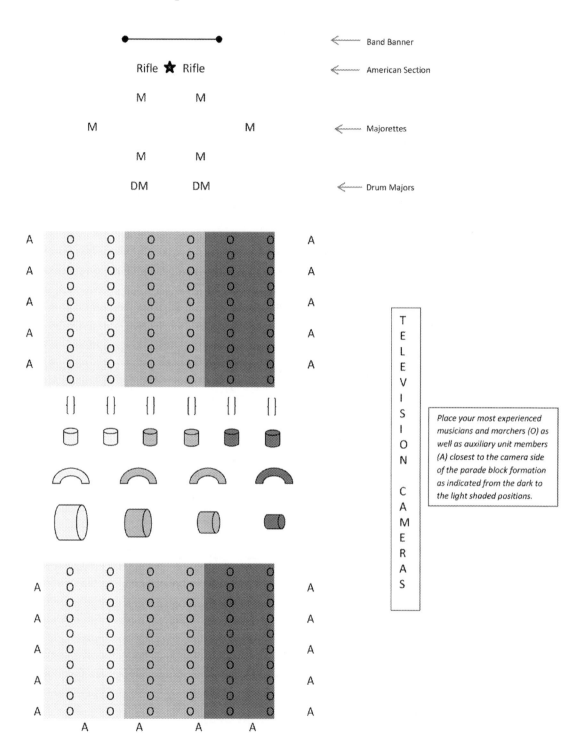

Rifle ★ Rifle

M   M

M   M

M   M

DM   DM

⟵ Band Banner

⟵ American Section

⟵ Majorettes

⟵ Drum Majors

T E L E V I S I O N   C A M E R A S

Place your most experienced musicians and marchers (O) as well as auxiliary unit members (A) closest to the camera side of the parade block formation as indicated from the dark to the light shaded positions.

56 Passenger Bus Seating Diagram

DRIVER			Seat 2	Seat 1
Seat 6	Seat 5		Seat 4	Seat 3
Seat 10	Seat 9		Seat 8	Seat 7
Seat 14	Seat 13		Seat 12	Seat 11
Seat 18	Seat 17		Seat 16	Seat 15
Seat 22	Seat 21		Seat 20	Seat 19
Seat 26	Seat 25		Seat 24	Seat 23
Seat 30	Seat 29	AISLE	Seat 28	Seat 27
Seat 34	Seat 33		Seat 32	Seat 31
Seat 38	Seat 37		Seat 36	Seat 35
Seat 42	Seat 41		Seat 40	Seat 39
Seat 46	Seat 45		Seat 44	Seat 43
Seat 50	Seat 49		Seat 48	Seat 47
Seat 54	Seat 53		Seat 52	Seat 51
Seat 56	Seat 55		RESTROOM	

Certificate of Insurance
Travel Agents and Tour Operators
Professional Liability Insurance

UNDERWRITTEN BY
(_____) INSURANCE COMPANY

This is to certify that the insurance policies specified below have been issued by (_____) INSURANCE COMPANY to the insured named herein and that, subject to their provisions, exclusions and conditions, such policies afford the coverage's indicated insofar as such coverage's apply to the occupation or business of the Named Insured as stated.

Name of Insured: (_____) Travel Company

Address: (_____)

                       (_____)

Location of Operations: Worldwide

Type of work covered: Travel Agency and Tour Operator Operations

Policy Number: (XXX XXXXXXX-XX)

Policy Period: From(XX/XX/XXXX) to (XX/XX/XXXX)
                   12:01 AM: standard time at the address of the named insured as stated herein.

	Coverage's	Limits of Liability	
A.	Bodily Injury and Property Damage	each occurrence	$2,000,000
B.	Bodily Injury and Property Damage Automobile (except owned automobile)	each occurrence	$2,000,000
C.	Professional Liability	each negligent act or negligent omission	$2,000,000
D.	Personal Injury	each offense	$2,000,000
	General Aggregate Limit:		$2,000,000
	Fire Legal Liability (if applicable)	Any one fire	$50,000

This Certificate Issued To:

(_____) INSURANCE COMPANY

Countersignature: _____

DATE: (XXXX XX, XXXX)   (if required by law)   Authorized Representative

CERTIFICATE HOLDER IS INCLUDED AS AN ADDITIONAL INSURED BUT ONLY WITH RESPECT TO THE NEGLIGENCE OF THE NAMED INSURED IN CONNECTION WITH THE TRAVEL AND/ OR TOUR SERVICES PROVIDED.

Butler Golden Tornado Band Resume

November	27, 1997	71st Macy's Thanksgiving Day Parade—Lead Band / NYC, New York
March	18, 1998	St. Patrick's Day Parade / Pittsburgh, Pennsylvania
April	29, 1999	Kentucky Derby Festival Pegasus Parade / Lexington, Kentucky
November	27, 1999	Celebrate the Seasons Parade / Pittsburgh, Pennsylvania
December	31, 1999	Disneyland Holiday Parade / Anaheim, California
January	1, 2000	111th Tournament of Roses Parade / Pasadena, California
November	19, 2000	Santa Claus Parade / Toronto, Canada
December	29, 2001	Florida Citrus Parade / Orlando, Florida
December	30, 2001	Disney World Holiday Parade / Orlando, Florida
November	28, 2002	77th Macy's Thanksgiving Day Parade / New York, New York
November	27, 2003	Boscov's Thanksgiving Day Parade / Philadelphia, Pennsylvania
December	31, 2004	Fort McDowell Fiesta Bowl Parade / Phoenix, Arizona
November	20, 2005	Santa Claus Parade / Toronto, Canada
January	1, 2007	118th Tournament of Roses Parade / Pasadena, California
November	11, 2007	Nation's Day Parade / New York, New York
December	29, 2008	Disney World Spectro Magic Parade / Orlando, Florida
December	30, 2008	Florida Citrus Parade / Orlando, Florida
November	26, 2009	IKEA Thanksgiving Day Parade / Philadelphia, Pennsylvania
December	31, 2010	Fort McDowell Fiesta Bowl Parade / Phoenix, Arizona
November	24, 2011	McDonald's Thanksgiving Day Parade / Chicago, Illinois

Butler Golden Tornado Band taking a group photo before
the 2010 Fort McDowell Fiesta Bowl Parade.
Photo by Jeff Groves